D0553638

BOSTON BAPTIST COLLEGE
LIBRARY
950 METROPOLITAN AVENUE
BOSTON,MA 02136
TEL (617) 364-3510 EXT 220

FUNDAMENTALS OF HEDGE FUND INVESTING

FUNDAMENTALS OF HEDGE FUND INVESTING

A PROFESSIONAL INVESTOR'S GUIDE

WILLIAM J. CREREND

McGraw-Hill

New York   San Francisco   Washington, D.C.   Auckland   Bogotá
Caracas   Lisbon   London   Madrid   Mexico City   Milan
Montreal   New Delhi   San Juan   Singapore
Sydney   Tokyo   Toronto

BOSTON BAPTIST COLLEGE
LIBRARY
950 METROPOLITAN AVENUE
BOSTON,MA 02136
TEL (617) 364-3510 EXT 216

Library of Congress Cataloging-in-Publication Data

Crerend, William J.
    Fundamentals of hedge fund investing : a professional investor's
guide / William J. Crerend.
      p. cm.
    ISBN 0-07-013522-3
    1. Hedge funds. I. Title.
    HG4530.C74   1998
    332.64'5—dc21   97-43914
                                        CIP

McGraw-Hill

A Division of The McGraw·Hill Companies

Copyright © 1998 by The McGraw-Hill Companies, Inc. All rights reserved. Printed in the
United States of America. Except as permitted under the United States Copyright Act of 1976,
no part of this publication may be reproduced or distributed in any form or by any means, or
stored in a data base or retrieval system, without the prior written permission of the publisher.

2 3 4 5 6 7 8 9 0   DOC/DOC   9 0 3 2 1 0 9 8

ISBN 0-07-013522-3

The sponsoring editor for this book was Jeffrey Krames, the editing supervisor was Donna
Namorato, and the production supervisor was Suzanne W. B. Rapcavage. It was set in Palatino
by Hendrickson Creative Communications of Oak Park, Illinois.

Printed and bound by R. R. Donnelley & Sons Company.

This publication is designed to provide accurate and authoritative information in regard to the
subject matter covered. It is sold with the understanding that neither the author nor the publisher
is engaged in rendering legal, accounting, or other professional service. If legal advice or other
expert assistance is required, the services of a competent professional person should be sought.

             —From a Declaration of Principles jointly adopted by a Committee of
               the American Bar Association and a Committee of Publishers.

Certain information contained herein is based on data and information supplied by investment
managers. The accuracy and completeness of such information and data have not been independently verified or approved by the author, and the author makes no representations with
respect thereto. Any statements of opinion constitute only current opinions of the author,
which are subject to change and which the author does not undertake to update. Nothing herein constitutes advice or an offer, solicitation, or endorsement with respect to any investment
area or vehicle. Due to, among other things, the volatile nature of the markets and the investment areas discussed herein, they are suitable only for certain investors. Parties should independently investigate any investment area or manager and should consult with qualified
investment, legal, and tax professionals before making any investment. Past performance is not
necessarily indicative of future results.

McGraw-Hill books are available at special quantity discounts to use as premiums and sales
promotions, or for use in corporate training programs. For more information, please write to
the Director of Special Sales, McGraw-Hill, 11 West 19th Street, New York, NY 10011. Or con-
tact your local bookstore.

This book is printed on acid-free paper.

CONTENTS

PREFACE

This book is written for investors wishing to gain a basic understanding of a world very often hidden from view. Too little has been written and, as a result, too little understood about an area that holds potential as a component of sophisticated, diversified investment programs. Although the subject of hedge funds may hold specific interest for experienced individual and institutional investors, anyone supervising the investment of assets should be intrigued. The book attempts to demystify hedge funds enough so that people retain a healthy respect for them but lose some of their fears as well.

To come away from this book smitten by a world "beyond understanding," or to conclude that the subject is too frightening to contemplate, is to miss the point completely. Hedge funds àre a class of investment that attracts many extraordinary professionals. Some have indeed become "legends" but not all fit that stereotype, and by the way, some traditional equity managers can similarly be described.

Hedge funds hide few real mysteries if you are willing to devote the time and diligence to study the players, their strategies, and the investment itself. Merit drives investment decisions and keeps open the mind of a great analyst.

Most of the topics in this book are covered generically and without specific reference to Evaluation Associates (EAI) and Evaluation Associates Capital Markets (EACM), the consulting firm and fund of funds operation, respectively, that the author works for and whose very businesses are investment services for large institutional funds and high-net-worth individuals. The exhibits and data representing the various hedge fund strategies are based on EACM's manager universes, which incorporate more than 400 series of manager returns, some with as much as 10 years history.

I also wish to acknowledge the help of my associates Anna Meena, Jody Grasty, Tony Minopoli, and Sally Marcus in the preparation of this book. I extend particular thanks to my partner and friend Tracey Hayes for her insight and advice, and to Janet Kalwat for critiquing and editing the manuscript.

My special thanks to my friend and partner Bob Jaeger for his help from start to finish. We had planned to co-author this book, but his business travel and responsibilities more neatly eased him into the role of chief advisor. It is a better effort because of him.

We would like to add a special, but anonymous, thanks to those hedge fund managers who helped me reach back through the years and who also gave me a glimpse into their souls. I knew and respected them as professionals in the field, and now I know them better as human beings.

William J. Crerend

INTRODUCTION

Depending on whom you talk to, hedge funds seem to have their roots in the 1930s, but they probably formally broke ground with A. W. Jones in the late 1940s. Growth was slow but steady going through the 1950s, and only in the mid-1960s did the bones of the business begin to gain some flesh. The late 1960s and early 1970s, with their treacherous markets, were more than a little troublesome, and it was not until the 1980s that the fledgling business regained its stride and experienced real growth.

Concurrent with those early days, some Wall Street trading desks were following a similar, albeit different, evolutionary path. Because they operated with proprietary capital, strategies and results had no formal structure, much less publicity. Even when firm capital gave way to block desk positioning, and investment banking and outside clients designated funds for management, limited communications surrounded the strategies offered, and meaningful explanations of results in terms of performance attribution basically did not exist.

As such, when people left "the Street" to start what we now call hedge funds, limited disclosure defined the culture of this emergent style of investment management. The fact that hedge fund managers were not registered with regulatory bodies, and accordingly could not advertise or offer their services publicly, only intensified the limited disclosure element, not to mention the proprietary nature of the strategies themselves.

Such was, and is, fertile ground for the rugged individualist. But to believe that current-day hedge fund managers are superhuman beings, as conventional wisdom might suggest, is to fail to understand the business. Though some are "gunslingers" and others "professors," most simply have great faith in themselves and their abilities, demand control of the investment process, and are intense and passionate about delivering performance results. Many hedge fund managers, in fact, represent a natural evolution from traditional asset management, having taken advantage of opportunities afforded by a long-lasting bull market to test their skills in new investment frontiers.

In the past, hedge fund investing has been the province of high net worth individuals. We believe we are on the edge of an institutional awakening to this area and, as such, to a huge change in its dynamics. With the exception of manager names, finding and evaluating hedge funds is difficult at best and often outside the experience of even the most practiced professional consultants, fund sponsors, and high net worth investors. But if return and diversification are common investor goals, and if hedge funds are the right place, how does the investor connect the relatively unknown world of hedge funds with the all too public world of institutional asset management? That is the subject of this text, but with an important caveat. Hedge funds are a wonderful, albeit small, part of the investment business, but they are not for everyone.

The progression of asset classes along the path of institutional acceptability is a subject unto itself. We diverge here, not to give a definitive view on the matter, but to offer some perspective on hedge funds versus other types of investments and their future role in institutional portfolios.

The following time line demonstrates the expansion across types of assets that institutional total portfolios have generally experienced over recent decades:

For reasons related to the market environment or inherent in the investment itself, asset classes have met various levels of success or degrees of integration into an institutional portfolio. International equity has grown so rapidly in acceptance—a function of the globalization of world markets—that it is rare to find an institutional portfolio today without significant foreign stock market exposure. Venture capital, on the other hand, has generally gained acceptance as an asset class but appears only as a small component of relatively few institutional funds. Farmland, at the other extreme, emerged and faltered as a viable investment area for institutions.

Asset class strategies typically (but not necessarily) move in sequence from nontraditional, to alternative, and finally to traditional status. An institutional portfolio usually contains representative strategies from each, as well as some in a "nowhere" category that includes collectibles, physical ownership of commodities, and direct ownership and operation of plant and equipment. (To infer that strategies in the latter group are unimportant is wrong, however, since they may have wide acceptance elsewhere.)

Nontraditional refers to investments other than time-honored assets such as stocks, bonds, and cash and often is the category where most asset classes start. Because of their historical conservative image, bonds probably never were nontraditional investments, whereas stocks and money markets warranted the designation to the extent that fiduciary funds did not invest in stocks, and money market funds did not exist. Believe it or not, U.S. stocks were a "nowhere" category for institutions in the 1950s in that such investors generally regarded stocks as too risky for fiduciary funds. Current examples of investments some might consider nontraditional are emerging markets debt, oil and gas, and various hedge fund strategies. Most important, some asset classes may never gain enough acceptance from institutions to move out of nontraditional status.

Alternative strategies are those that have gained more acceptance than nontraditional but may never make it to traditional status, for some or all of the following reasons:

1. *Size (liquidity)*. An inherent inability to absorb significant assets may prohibit the asset class from constituting a substantial portion of an institutional fund. A number of hedge fund strategies are restrictive in this sense.

2. *Seasoning*. Some asset classes passing through to traditional status need considerable time for fund sponsors to develop a sense of understanding and confidence. Emerging markets equity, for example, currently is in a transitional stage as improving research, data availability, and custody arrangements lessen some of the risks associated with this asset class.

3. *Legal/regulatory*. Dating back to the concepts of "legal lists" and "basket provisions," some otherwise attractive and accepted asset classes are relegated to junior varsity status by charter or applicable rules. Given the need to "lock up" funds for as much as 15 years, private equity is one such restricted investment that may, in fact, remain "alternative" indefinitely.

4. *Volatility*. Return volatility or even the perception of a relatively low success ratio within the individual investments of the asset class itself may commit the strategy to "alternative" status. Venture capital partnerships may fall into this category as a potentially good investment but with a limited hit ratio of substantial successes therein.

5. *"By Nature."* Some asset classes, while attractive, are simply too esoteric to be a major part of a total fund. As Keynes observed, "It is better to fail conventionally than to succeed unconventionally." Again, many of the hedge fund strategies fall into this category.

Traditional status imparts the idea of main-line, liquid, and understandable performance, which together characterize the dominant parts of an institutional total fund. Membership in this club is not preordained: almost any asset class that meets the requisite tests (or overcomes the prohibitive factors outlined above) can join the big leagues.

Our time line indicates that hedge funds are in the early stages of recognition and acceptance by institutions. Though hedge funds have been in existence for some 50 years, institutions historically have abhorred the shorting and use of leverage and derivatives that typically accompany such strategies. As institutions expanded their use of asset classes, they more often sought out other alternative strategies (such as international or emerging markets equity) that were more natural extensions of their current investment strategies and that also were better able to accommodate large institutional assets. Given that a growing number of institutions are just now becoming more comfortable with hedge funds, it is too early to predict how these large investors will ultimately accept and use this asset class. One of the defining characteristics of hedge funds is their lack of homogeneity. That is, over time, some hedge fund strategies will be more capable of absorbing large assets than others and some will prove more "acceptable" than others in different ways. To add to the complexity, hedge fund strategies use many of the other categories of investments, be they nontraditional, alternative, or traditional.

Keep in mind that the terms *nontraditional* and *alternative* are somewhat arbitrary. The less the acceptance of the asset class, regardless of terminology, the greater the ineffi-ciencies or price imperfections in the marketplace that buy-ers or sellers can use to their advantage as a result of greater insight or information, or some other edge. To maximize the potential for superior returns, it is thus best to evaluate asset classes as early in the progression path toward traditional status as possible.

We have already warned that hedge funds are not for the faint of heart. From the start, note that unlike traditional man-agers, hedge funds can lose more than 100% in a day. This book is thus written for the sole purpose of conveying infor-mation about the area, not to tout it. With that said, some of us enjoy and respect the inherent potential in such an entre-preneurial business. Our enthusiasm can be contagious, so keep your guard up and your skepticism in full bloom.

FUNDAMENTALS OF HEDGE FUND INVESTING

CHAPTER 1

What Are Hedge Funds? Why Invest in Them?

WHAT ARE HEDGE FUNDS?

In the past, the term *hedge fund* typically referred to an unregistered investment adviser—that is, one not registered with the Securities and Exchange Commission and therefore not subject to its regulations. The term was also associated with the practice of buying and selling U.S. stocks and bonds on a leveraged basis and with holding both long positions (buying and selling securities you own) and short positions (selling securities you borrow with the expectation of replacing them at lower prices). In general, hedge funds derived their name from the fact that they were often long and short, thus "hedged" or protected to some degree against market uncertainties.

Today, hedge funds encompass not just long, short, and levered securities but also futures (contracts for commodities or more often financial instruments bought or sold for delivery at a future date), forwards (similar to futures but not exchange traded), options (the right to buy or sell something else), and even physicals (tangible assets such as wheat, oil, copper, and gold). However expansive the term, hedge fund investing remains essentially the same. That is, you are long something because you believe the price will rise and short something because you believe the price will decline, and if you are really certain, you will borrow money to do either or both.

A number of descriptors exist, but they oversimplify hedge funds. For example, "Hedge fund managers are aggressive investors" is generally true, but they can also be very conservative. Another, "You can expect very high returns," is in no way guaranteed and, further, is not always the goal. Finally, a favorite, "They charge high fees, often performance related," is almost universally true but ignores the more important consideration of net returns to the investor.

In and of itself, "hedge funds" is not a homogeneous grouping. There are many approaches or strategies at work here, and differentiating among them will aid in understanding them. At the outset, keep in mind that hedge fund managers have a broad palette, perhaps the broadest in the investment management business. Terms like *growth* or *value*, *small* or *large*, *domestic* or *foreign*, *stocks* or *bonds* have limited use as defining characteristics because hedge fund managers span many types of investments, markets, sectors, and styles in search of returns.

As a point of departure, remember that traditional investing focuses on ownership of stocks and bonds—that is, long positions in financial assets. Hedge fund investing opens up a new world of opportunities in its extension to nonfinancial assets, and shorting and leveraging techniques. As the complexity of hedge fund strategies increases, so does the level of caution in understanding and assessing their potential risks and returns.

Let us begin then by differentiating five broad categories of hedge funds.

TYPES OF HEDGE FUNDS

Relative Value

Sometimes referred to as market-neutral strategies, Relative Value portfolios are the only strategies primarily focused on linking specific positions in a "hedged" fashion. These portfolios, which combine long positions and offsetting short positions, seek returns independent of market movements while extracting returns from mispriced securities, market sectors, or groups of securities. Relative Value strategies attempt to limit market or "systematic" risk while taking advantage of inefficiencies between asset classes or securities. Perfect hedging, of course, is rarely if ever possible in attempting to extract investment returns, so be realistic in your expectations. Notwithstanding the historical consistency of returns, hedging is an art rather than a science.

To give you some examples, a Relative Value portfolio might be long 25 undervalued U.S. technology stocks and short 25 overvalued U.S. technology stocks; long IBM convertible bonds and short an appropriate amount of IBM stock; or long a cheap basket of warrants on Japanese stocks and short a comparable amount of futures on the Japanese stock market. Essentially, the manager buys undervalued securities and shorts overvalued securities, hoping that the long positions outperform the short positions, or vice versa. In the worst case, possibly a sharp market action, the manager's long positions may decline while the short positions rise, resulting in losses on both sides. In the best case, the long positions rise while the short positions fall. This outbreak from the initial balanced position results in a spread return, generally known as "alpha." Relative Value managers seek to maximize a positive alpha.

The desired rate of return for a Relative Value portfolio, more modest than for other hedge fund strategies, is 3% to 5% per year above the risk-free three-month U.S. Treasury bill (net of fees) with relatively low volatility. If Relative Value over- or underperforms the S&P 500 or other stock market indices, it is more of an accident than anything else. Yet market or macro factors certainly can affect this strategy. Still, when investing in Relative Value, you should seek returns above the risk-free rate and focus on that target over the long term.

Within the Relative Value category, we further distinguish four approaches.

Long/Short Equity—Long Undervalued Equities/Short Overvalued Equities

This strategy, popular with institutions given its likeness to traditional stock picking analysis, is perhaps the most intuitively appealing, since it combines long positions in stocks you think are undervalued with short positions in those you think are overvalued, typically balancing the portfolio structure by consideration of markets, sectors, industries, market capitalization sizes, and other differentiating characteristics. Whether by fundamental, technical, or quantitative techniques, long/short equity attempts to factor out market and sectoral factors, leaving only the inefficiencies of stock selection, and your identification thereof, as a source of portfolio return.

Some approaches balance the dollar amount long against the dollar amount short, while others attempt to balance the estimated volatility of the longs and the shorts. Still others utilize computer-driven models with over 50 factors or elements to balance. The more complex the system, the more the implied certainty, yet the more difficult it is to analyze and correct should something go wrong. To add to the complexity, portfolios could be 30 names long and 30 names short, or 100 both ways.

Though seemingly much to manage and maintain, long/short equity portfolios are not that difficult to understand conceptually. For example, if a portfolio is long 20 U.S. regional bank stocks and short 20 U.S. regional bank stocks in equal dollar amounts, the bet is, for the most part, on stock selection. The possibility exists, of course, that the longs go south and the shorts go north, so that the portfolio never can be perfectly hedged. If you leave the long positions in regional bank stocks but change the short positions to money center bank stocks, the portfolio becomes less neutral and appears to reflect two different bets. Changing the shorts to regional Canadian banks lessens the hedge even further. Finally, applying the shorts to U.S. retail companies increases the bet and changes the nature of the portfolio entirely.

Complicated? Perhaps so, but portfolio managers often see more science than art to the process while we view it more the other way. At the end of the day, it's always a judgment call.

Convertible Hedging—Long Convertible Bonds/Short Underlying Common Stock
This variant of Relative Value buys a convertible bond (or other type of convertible instrument such as preferred stock) and then shorts an appropriate amount of the same company's stock to make it a hedged transaction. Consider the following example:

Buy	1	ABC Corp 7% 2002 convertible bond	Current price: 1000
Sell	22	ABC Corp common stock	Current price: 35

The above transaction implies a *hedge ratio* of 77%—that is, a purchase of a $1000 bond offset by the simultaneous short sale of 22 shares of ABC stock at $35, or $770. This hedge ratio is important, because it refers to that amount of the stock that is required to offset price fluctuation in the bond. In our example, for every $1 that the stock moves, the bond is expected to move by $0.77.

Adding the components of the return, the investor would earn coupon interest on the bond of $70 (7% of the $1000 face value). Additionally, brokers will pay interest on the proceeds from the short sale of stock, generally equal to the three-month T-bill rate. If T-bills yield 5% and the short position is 70% of capital, then there is an additional 3.5% of yield. Assuming no dividends are owed on the stock sold and no market movement occurs, the total return would be 10.5% (7% plus an effective 3.5% rebate, after adjusting for the amount hedged). The trade becomes potentially more lucrative for those who employ leverage to boost the return: In our example, a 7% borrowing cost would yield an additional 3.5% for each unit of leverage.

Notwithstanding, the convertible hedger seeks to make money by adjusting the hedge ratio accordingly, given favorable or adverse market movements. If the underlying stock goes up, the bond will generally increase in value and will become more sensitive to further increases in the value of the stock, thus requiring a larger short stock position to hedge the long bond position. The convertible hedger thus tends to be shorting more stock as stock prices rise, giving a "contrarian" bias to his trading behavior. As the stock declines, the hedge ratio may be appropriately set at lower levels, where the bond's behavior is less volatile and more characteristic of interest rate instruments and their sensitivities. (See Exhibit 1–1.)

E X H I B I T   1-1

Required Hedge Ratio

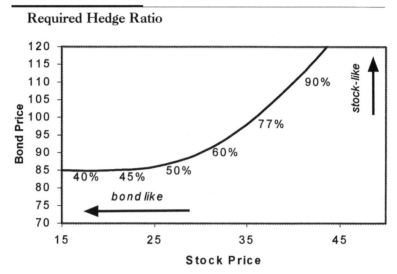

Remember that the convertible investment is often a bond and, as such, independently affected by interest rate movements and features of the bond such as maturity, credit quality, and call protection; the stock, on the other hand, is subject to market and industry/sector movements. If a takeover attempt occurs, the stock price could be bid up (and you are short), and if it is a leveraged takeover (weakening the balance sheet), the bond price could decline (and you are long). Obviously, the trade is not, and never can be, a lockup of return.

Bond Hedging—Yield Curve Arbitrage or Long/Short Debt Positions
Bond hedging is the art of being long a higher-yielding fixed income instrument and short another at a lower yield (only

the valiant do this for capital gains), maintaining as close to
a hedged position as humanly possible. One such trade could
be a long position in a three-year U.S. Treasury note and a
short position in one as close to that maturity as possible,
levered significantly because the spread between the two is
hardly worth the trade otherwise. Or the manager might
exploit yield differences between different market sectors,
e.g., mortgages versus Treasuries or corporates versus
Treasuries. Other trades could be long a three-year Treasury
note and short a two-year and a four-year, or long a three-year
U.S. Treasury and short a similar maturity non-U.S. sovereign credit. The latter transaction requires a view on currencies and the application of appropriate currency hedges to
provide protection against future exchange rate fluctuations.
One such method is to buy or sell currencies in the forward
market in which currencies are exchanged at a designated
future date at an agreed-upon price.

What could go wrong? Everything! Markets are unpre-
dictable. For reasons known only to the buyer, someone
might need vast quantities of the bond you are short, making your hedge go haywire. Or the yield curve could twist
right between the two maturities you own. Or the currency
hedge could fail because the currency moved out of the
expected band.

Rotational—Multiple Relative Value Strategies
Rotational managers move across the Relative Value strategies opportunistically, as well as across other strategies not
likely to be used on a stand-alone basis. The latter might
include hedging spreads between commodities such as crude
versus gasoline or spot gold versus gold futures, or combining long positions in closed-end funds with shorts in the constituent stocks.

Event Driven

Event Driven strategies are long-biased strategies that focus on specific corporate transactions that are likely to produce a reasonably well-defined increase in the value of a security within a reasonably well-defined time horizon. While the traditional value-oriented investor will invest in a company because he believes that his investment will appreciate substantially over the long haul, the event driven investor has a more specific idea of the size of the gain, and the timing of the gain. The corporate transactions in question fall into two main areas: the risk arbitrage investor focuses on equity-related opportunities created by mergers, acquisitions, tender offers, and related situations, while the distressed debt specialist focuses on opportunities created by bankruptcies, liquidations, financial reorganizations, and the like. Since event driven strategies are directed toward specific transactions that have "a beginning, a middle, and an end," returns are often quite independent of broad market movements.

To illustrate risk arbitrage, suppose that company ABC has an interest in acquiring company XYZ, which is trading in the marketplace at a price of $50 per share. Acquisition-minded companies are typically willing to pay premiums of 30% or more to the pre-deal price, which means that ABC may be willing to pay $65 per share for XYZ. When ABC announces a $65 bid for XYZ, the price of XYZ will rise rapidly, but may not hit $65, since the deal may not happen, or the timing may become delayed. (On the other hand, the price may move above $65 if the market anticipates that higher bids will emerge.) The risk arbitrageur is constantly weighing three questions: (1) What is the probability that the deal will go through?; (2) If the deal happens, what will be the final price for XYZ?; (3) If the deal happens, when will it happen?

Distressed debt investing requires a somewhat similar analysis. If the investor owns the debt of a company undergoing financial reorganization, there are three key questions: (1) What is the probability that the company will be successfully reorganized (and not liquidated)?; (2) If the company is reorganized, what package of securities will the bondholders receive, and what will they be worth?; (3) When will the transaction be finalized?

Most investors approach the event driven area with return expectations of 15% or more, plus the expectation of some lack of correlation with broad market moves. At the time of this writing, deal arbitrage is thriving in terms of the number of deals, but spreads (the difference between market value and the bid price of a target company's stock) are not necessarily lucrative. Although participating in the right deal (one that will be consummated) is vital, you also want to make sufficient money to justify the investment over the limited time you are in it. Curiously, deal arbitrage is one of the few hedge fund strategies with specific industry data available, such as the current number of deals, spreads, industries involved, and type of transaction (stock, cash, etc.).

Event Driven strategies are more complicated than most people know. In mergers and acquisitions, stocks can be bid up rapidly to a price close to or above the one an acquirer offers to pay. An Event Driven manager must quickly make a judgment as to the possible rate of return available if the deal goes through (or if a higher competing bid emerges), and the potential for a collapse in the stock price if the deal fails or is withdrawn. If a large position has been taken, it can be very difficult to sell if a deal fails and the stock plummets. In a bankruptcy situation, the manager who has done in-depth research might determine that a certain tranche of bonds looks attractive because they are collateralized by an unrecognized, valuable asset (such as a fleet of aircraft in an otherwise ailing airline company), while less astute bond-holders are selling at distressed prices because of the impending bankruptcy. Similarly, careful analysis of a distressed company might show assets, undervalued by others, that actually are adequate to cover senior debt obligations. Again, the shrewd manager buys while others sell in fright, and perhaps even shorts some same-company stock to hedge the bond position. In other words, exiting of investments by traditional managers actually creates opportunities for deal arbitrage and distressed investing.

Deal arbitrage and distressed investing are not naturally "joined at the hip," since there are partnerships that specialize in each. Still, because definite cycles exist for each and do not necessarily correlate, it has often been good business to diversify by using both approaches. Whether used separately or in combination, Event Driven strategies are deeply rooted in good research and strong convictions, because they are often performed when existing owners are moving to the exit.

Equity Hedge Funds

Equity Hedge funds, the third category we consider, invest in equity securities both long and short but unlike Relative Value portfolios, these portfolios will generally have some net market exposure, usually in the long direction. You might consider these managers the original hedge fund managers, flowing from traditional stock-picking backgrounds into the use of strategies that combine long investing (sometimes using leverage) with some short positions to reflect their opinions but also to exercise what they believe to be a market hedge. Given their traditional portfolio management backgrounds,

Equity Hedge fund managers typically operate with certain style biases such as small capitalization or concentrations in financial or technology stocks.

To label Equity Hedge fund managers as market timers, as conventional wisdom might suggest, is incorrect. These managers are stock pickers at heart, driven by fundamental company research. Equity Hedge fund managers pride themselves on analytic ability: They like to buy strong, growing, or turnaround companies at a good price, particularly if Wall Street hasn't yet identified the stocks as attractive. Although they short the stocks that will "probably perform poorly," the short side tends to expand materially when markets run up to values deemed unreasonable, and may not otherwise be a significant part of the portfolio under normal conditions. The short side, for the most part, evolves both by stock selection and a sense of risk aversion to the portfolio or market as a whole. Equity Hedge managers do not seek to outperform the market in the short term, but they usually expect to outperform it over the long term as a result of their good absolute returns.

As a broad category, Equity Hedge funds encompass three subcategories: domestic long biased, domestic opportunistic (manager may be net short), and global/international, which vary according to use of U.S. versus non-U.S. stocks as well as the degree to which shorting is utilized. As a whole, the strategy has a 15%± goal for total annual rate of return net of fees.

Global Asset Allocators

Global Asset Allocators, our fourth category, invest worldwide and utilize almost any strategy with both long and short positions in securities, futures, forwards, options, and physical commodities. Otherwise referred to as commodity trading advisers (CTAs), macro hedge funds, or futures traders, Global Asset Allocators include those managers that get most of the attention in the popular press by virtue of their total asset size, often enormous positions, and established reputations. In at least one dimension, Global Asset Allocators are the big brother of Equity Hedge funds. With tremendous Wall Street trading power and leverage behind their successful businesses, some of the Equity Hedge funds have grown so large as to need to broaden their palette, and therein lies the difficulty. Can a $300 million Equity Hedge fund grow to $3 billion in size and still do the same things? The answer is probably no, given that reasonably liquid positions in individual issues (such as small capitalization stocks) are prohibitive at such size, driving these "giants" into other asset classes and markets. One group of managers that fall into this category are the former "commodity" managers. Having outgrown the capacity of the markets for physical commodities (in large size, a single fund can *become* the market in commodity trading), they have moved rapidly into financial futures and currency markets.

To call Global Asset Allocators market timers is to understate the complexity of what managers of this strategy do. The timing of diverse markets certainly can be an integral part of their approach, which some do by technical (price momentum) as opposed to fundamental (individual company or market) research. The aforementioned "commodity managers" tend to dominate the technical approaches, while fundamentalists are more the true global hedge funds (some strategies combine both approaches). Whether technical or fundamental in orientation, Global Asset Allocators use just about everything and go just about anywhere to get the job done. What is the goal for these managers? A total annual return of 15% to 20% (net of fees) is generally the target.

As you consider the demands of global investing, keep in mind that in most instances an investment in a non-U.S. instrument requires a currency translation (selling dollars to buy Japanese yen, for example, and then using the yen to buy a stock, bond, or other instrument). To sell a position, you need to reverse the transaction. There are thus two decisions involved in buying and selling non-U.S. investments: the investment itself and the currency. Indeed, many Global Asset Allocators will take positions in currencies alone, at times with large leverage. As such, these managers warrant the name *macro hedge funds*, because their portfolios hold positions that reflect not only bets on the fortunes of individual companies and/or sectors but also bets on the fortunes of countries and currencies themselves, and even regions such as the European Economic Community (EEC) or the prospective European Monetary System (EMS). Bets of the latter type can place Global Asset Allocators in agreement or disagreement with governments and sovereign central banks and, at times, in great size.

Global Asset Allocators are portfolio managers who have grown in assets, inquisitiveness, intellect, and experience to grapple with the most diverse and complex global investment challenges of the day.

Short Selling

Short Selling is the reverse of conventional wisdom, in terms of the trade. Here, managers sell securities they don't own, expecting to buy them back at lower prices. Shorting is a serious, complicated process to negotiate and maintain. You need to open a margin account with a broker in which the deposited cash or securities serve as collateral against price changes that go against the short. The broker typically borrows from a customer who never knows the stock is gone, because it continues to be valued at market on the brokerage statements and, of course, any dividends payable are paid (by the borrower) to the account as well. The proceeds of the sale of the borrowed stock are kept in the short seller's account and earn interest, which is shared by the broker and the short seller. The short seller pays the requisite dividends, if any, out of pocket to the account of the customer who owns the stock sold short. If the stock falls in price, the short seller can buy the security at the market and replace it at a profit in the account from which it was borrowed. If it rises in price, the short seller may be subject to a loss and a *margin call* from the broker, requiring the short seller to put more assets in his account. If necessary, the seller could buy the security at the then market price to cover the short or close the position. If the owning customer decides to sell the heretofore borrowed security while the short remains on, the broker either borrows it from another place or, failing that, forces the short seller to buy the security at the market value and cover the short, possibly at a loss.

Although Short Selling is used to greater or lesser extents in all of the above strategies, it also can be a stand-alone strategy. Short sellers are people who take a great deal of professional (not personal) pleasure in finding as yet undiscovered fraud, gross overvaluations, and other negative company situations. Some people shun Short Selling as un-American or antibusiness, making short sales potentially very inefficient in investment terms and profitable for the relatively small subset of investors who pursue this strategy.

Short Selling takes a special breed of thinker, clearly someone looking and able to take advantage of unseen trouble before the world sees it. In effect, short sellers have to sell short before the negative news engulfs the security and it declines. To prevent short sellers from pushing prices down to enhance their own profitability, applicable rules for equities trading in certain markets specify that short sales must be made on an uptick (a price higher than that of the previous trade). In a plummeting situation, upticks are hard to find.

Dedicated short sellers are a somewhat rare and tenacious breed. Part of the reason has simply to do with the math. If you buy a security, and the stock goes to zero, the most you can lose is your investment, or stated another way, 100%. If you short a security that subsequently goes up in price, your loss can be many multiples of 100%. Keep in mind that if you short a stock and it goes against you, the stock becomes a larger part of the portfolio by virtue of its rise in value.

Return expectations for Short Selling are more a function of the markets than anything else. If the stock market declines a great deal, shorting can do very, very well; vice versa is equally true. In flat markets it is possible for short sellers to compete, but much depends on stock selection. In the current bull market, returns have suffered and short sellers strain to stay in business. Note that up until the last five or six years, short sellers have at least been able to survive in strong equity markets. More recently, the mutual fund-driven momentum of the bull markets has driven many short sellers out of business. Their demise is unfortunate, because short sellers are a balance to a "very complex flywheel" that would be missed. In other words, by exposing and exerting pressure on negative company situations, short sellers act as a kind of filtering process that benefits the entire market and economic environments.

The foregoing descriptions of the various hedge fund strategies indicate that a great deal of scope and breadth exists within and between them. A portfolio could hold 5 securities or 600. The 5-issue portfolio could be all long, all short, or some combination; the portfolio with 600 securities could have 300 long and 300 short positions. There could be a mixture of the U.S. and foreign, developed and developing markets, the latter of which might include the People's Republic of China or Russia. Independent of the markets, the instruments utilized might be stocks, bonds, convertibles, preferred stocks, asset-backed securities, and the like, as well as derivative forms such as futures, forwards, and swaps. Moreover, many of these instruments will emanate from countries with different laws and regulations from those in the United States.

Though most managers tend to adhere to their respective strategies, it is endemic to the hedge fund area for managers to drift into other strategies opportunistically. As such, Event Driven managers can invest in announced deals and/or bankruptcies with or without leverage, sometimes opportunistically hedging their position depending on the outlook. Equity Hedge funds differentiate themselves even more by degrees of leverage and their bias toward long or short positions. It goes without saying that the propensity to shift across strategies requires a tremendous dependence on manager knowledge, systems, and skills.

As a review, the following simple table provides one way of organizing the hedge fund universe:

Directional Bias	Strategy
long and short (balanced)	Relative Value
net long (more long than short) or net short (more short than long)	Opportunistic Equity Hedge; Global Asset Allocator
long bias	Event Driven; most Equity Hedge Funds
short bias	Short Selling

Having looked at the various hedge fund strategies, you might ask how many managers currently are associated with each, and which strategies have garnered the most assets. Based on a representative universe, Exhibit 1–2 shows the distribution of assets by strategy and size.

In a historical sense, Relative Value is a reasonably new and complex set of strategies. With the exception of long/short equity, the proportion of managers in the three other subsets is still small; typical asset sizes are in the $50–500 million range. Event Driven is an older strategy but with interest limited to a specialized group. Considered the granddaddy of hedge funds, Equity Hedge has attracted a large number of practitioners because it offers a natural entry point into the area for people coming out of traditional equity management. Within this group, domestic opportunistic has the fewest managers but a predominance of asset sizes greater than $1 billion. Global Asset Allocators have derived their large numbers from Equity Hedge funds that have outgrown the asset capacity of their strategies, as well as from the former commodity specialists who also have required a broader palette to operate. Notice that the majority of "discretionary" managers have assets greater than $1 billion. Finally, Short Selling, never the home of the stock picker in traditional investing, recently has been battered by poor performance and is more likely to suffer from attrition in the ranks than to grow further. These managers are characteristically smaller in asset size.

WHY INVEST IN HEDGE FUNDS?

The hope of above-average returns (absolute or relative to a benchmark), diversification from traditional asset classes, and possible downside protection are the real answers. Unfortunately, some include bragging and name dropping at cocktail parties among their reasons as well.

E X H I B I T   1-2

Distribution of Assets by Strategy and Size
As of December 31, 1996

| Strategy | Total Universe | | Strategy Assets Under Management: Size Ranges | | | | | | | |
	AUM $MM	Mgrs (Percent)	>$1B	$1B to $750MM	$750MM to $500MM	$500MM to $250MM	$250MM to $100MM	$100MM to $50MM	$50MM to $20MM	Under $20MM
			Percent of Strategy Assets Managed in Each Size Category							
Bond Hedge	$1,701	3 %	0.0 %	0.0	0.0 %	69.1 %	23.2 %	3.8 %	3.9 %	0.0 %
Convertible Hedge	$2,118	5	76.2	0.0	0.0	0.0	6.3	11.6	2.8	3.0
Long/Short Equity	$4,031	9	29.8	0.0	15.0	19.9	19.2	10.6	3.5	2.0
Rotational	$2,875	7	0.0	0.0	20.2	24.6	38.3	11.9	4.6	0.4
Relative Value	$10,724	24	26.2	0.0	11.0	25.0	22.4	10.1	3.7	1.5
Bankruptcy/Distressed	$5,797	7 %	21.1 %	12.9 %	38.8 %	11.7 %	6.9 %	5.2 %	3.1 %	0.3 %
Multi-Event	$3,906	3	29.4	23.8	30.5	0.0	11.5	3.6	1.1	0.0
Risk Arbitrage	$2,938	7	0.0	0.0	18.7	49.7	21.5	4.1	4.8	1.2
Event Driven	$12,641	18	18.8	13.3	31.5	16.9	11.7	4.5	2.9	0.4
Domestic Long Equity	$3,151	8 %	0.0 %	26.3 %	0.0 %	33.6 %	16.8 %	17.0 %	6.0 %	0.4 %
Domestic Opportunistic Equity	$3,821	4	62.8	0.0	0.0	16.9	15.2	1.9	2.9	0.2
Global/International	$6,796	12	0.0	24.7	19.1	30.5	16.6	7.0	1.4	0.6
Equity Hedge	$13,768	24	17.4	18.2	9.4	27.4	16.3	7.9	2.9	0.5
Discretionary	$30,831	13 %	80.9 %	5.9 %	2.1 %	5.5 %	4.7 %	0.6 %	0.1 %	0.2 %
Systematic	$6,595	15	33.6	0.0	16.7	15.8	20.8	6.0	5.2	1.9
Global Asset Allocators	$37,426	28	72.6	4.9	4.7	7.3	7.6	1.6	1.0	0.5
Short Selling	$1,120	6 %	0.0 %	0.0 %	0.0 %	35.4 %	45.0 %	12.9 %	1.8 %	4.9 %
Total Universe	$75,679	100 %	45.9 %	7.9 %	10.9 %	15.5 %	12.5 %	4.6 %	2.0 %	0.7 %

Source: EACM Alternative Strategy Universe.

19

Real or imagined, people think of hedge funds as having the potential for high returns, the patterns of which should be unlike any other asset they own. At the outset, be advised that complete and well-scrutinized performance data can be tough to come by in this area. Hearsay, tall tales, and subsequently misunderstanding and inaccuracy abound. Chapter 5 (Evaluating Hedge Funds) discusses performance issues in greater detail. Suffice it to say here that verification of hedge fund performance requires careful attention to disclosure issues, checks against audited results, pricing methods of unquoted securities, and the possibility of inappropriate manager groupings, as well as group averages that mask wide dispersion of returns.

As a beginning, Exhibit 1–3 compares the risk/return characteristics over a 10-year period for the five hedge fund strategies and several traditional asset classes. Throughout this book we use the S&P 500 Index to represent U.S. stocks,

E X H I B I T   1–3

Alternative Strategies vs. Traditional Strategies
Risk/Return Characteristics: 10 Years Ending 12/31/96

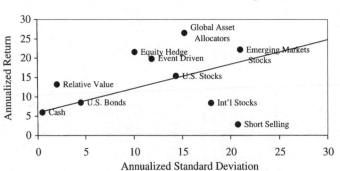

Sources: EACM Alternative Strategy Universes, Standard & Poor's, Morgan Stanley Capital International, Lehman Brothers, Merrill Lynch. Note: For this and subsequent exhibits, the return series for emerging markets stocks begins in 1988.

and the Morgan Stanley Capital International Europe, Australia, and Far East (MSCI EAFE) and Emerging Markets Free (MSCI EMF) indices to represent the stock markets of foreign developed and developing markets, respectively. We use the Lehman Brothers Aggregate Bond Index and the Merrill Lynch Three-Month Treasury Bill to represent U.S. bonds and cash, respectively. (Appendix I to this book contains details of all indices used.) The returns for the hedge fund strategies represent EACM manager universes, which consist of approximately 400 series of manager returns. The EACM data for each strategy reflect equally weighted monthly composites of these returns, net of all fees, from the period 1987 to 1996, including terminated managers within the group.

Over the period observed in Exhibit 1–3, only Short Selling had substantially higher volatility than the other nontraditional strategies, an unsurprising result given the nature of the strategy and the market environment of the time period measured. Equity Hedge, Event Driven, and Global Asset Allocators had returns substantially higher than U.S. and foreign stocks with less or similar volatility. (Note that the volatility of the composite will be less than the volatility of individual managers.) Keep in mind, however, that Exhibit 1–3 reflects only a single, past period and that group averages do not imply any certainty with regard to the returns of any given manager or sector (more on this subject in the next chapter).

We next examine similarities in patterns of returns between the hedge fund strategies and traditional asset classes by means of the correlation matrix in Exhibit 1–4. Remember that a correlation of +1.00 is a perfect positive correlation, meaning that the returns of any given two asset classes move in the same direction. A correlation of –1.00, a perfect inverse correlation, means that the two returns move

E X H I B I T   1–4

Correlation of Monthly Returns
10 Years Ending 12/31/96

	Relative Value	Event Driven	Equity Hedge	Global AA	Short Selling	U.S. Stocks	U.S. Bonds	Int'l Stocks	Emg Mkts Stocks	Cash
Relative Value	1.00									
Event Driven	0.00	1.00								
Equity Hedge	0.18	0.75	1.00							
Global AA	0.11	-0.05	0.03	1.00						
Short Selling	-0.03	-0.52	-0.69	0.12	1.00					
U.S. Stocks	0.04	0.61	0.79	0.02	-0.70	1.00				
U.S. Bonds	0.32	-0.11	0.09	0.08	-0.04	0.32	1.00			
Int'l Stocks	0.11	0.34	0.46	0.02	-0.38	0.48	0.09	1.00		
Emg Mkts Stocks	0.25	0.25	0.51	-0.10	-0.37	0.38	0.07	0.39	1.00	
Cash	0.30	-0.16	-0.08	0.19	0.20	-0.01	0.27	-0.08	0.02	1.00

Sources: EACM Alternative Strategy Universes, Standard & Poor's, Morgan Stanley Capital International, Lehman Brothers, Merrill Lynch.

in opposite directions. A correlation of zero implies that no relationship (of the linear type) exists between the returns.

Over the time period observed, Short Selling (–0.70) has a strong inverse correlation with U.S. stocks, while Global Asset Allocators (0.02) and Relative Value (0.04) have a low correlation with this asset class. Event Driven (0.61) and Equity Hedge (0.79) strategies, in contrast, exhibit a closer relationship to the market. Within hedge fund strategies themselves, note the overall low correlations and the range from –0.69 between Short Selling and Equity Hedge to 0.75 between Equity Hedge and Event Driven.

Though low correlations to U.S. stocks are desirable for diversification purposes, it is important to remember that relationships like Equity Hedge (0.79) could be close yet still offer some downside sensitivity; Global Asset Allocators (0.02) could be a "perfect unmatch" and Short Selling (–0.70)

a useful hedge. No guarantees exist, of course, for future relationships. Exhibit 1–4 provides only a quick take on what
has been and what might develop in the future.

Correlations and other means of examining relationships
among the returns of asset classes have important implications for portfolio diversification, which is important for managing risk. Unlikely as it may seem, if you own an Australian
government bond, a German auto stock, and a U.S. hedge
fund, your portfolio is *not* diversified if the three investments
have a similar pattern of returns. At the same time, perfect
inverse correlation cancels out gains and losses. The quest is
to employ a strategy biased toward an anticipated market
direction while endeavoring to dampen volatility of returns
through diversification.

Based on the possibility of attractively low correlations
between traditional and hedge fund strategies, Exhibits 1–5
and 1–6 suggest that you could have reduced risk and
increased return over the period observed by blending some
hedge fund strategies with the S&P 500 and MSCI EAFE,
respectively. (Note that in between the 100% ends of each
line are measured gradations mixing proportions of each
hedge fund strategy with the index.)

The introductory exhibits in this chapter lend support to
hedge funds as a component of a diversified total portfolio in
terms of return, volatility, and diversification. There is a long
way to go, however, since we have only begun to break down
"hedge funds" into broad categories and subdivisions. Simple
correlations and measures of volatility mask the particular
characteristics of each strategy, changes over time, the more
qualitative considerations, and, most important, the specific
features of the individual managers who ultimately provide the
returns. With this admonition, Chapter 2 begins the task.

E X H I B I T   1–5

Incremental Allocations of Alternative Strategies
to U.S. Stocks
10 Years Ending 12/31/96

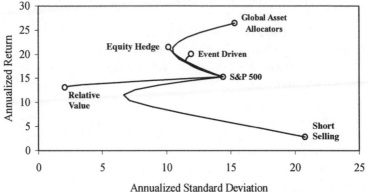

Annualized Standard Deviation

Source: EACM Alternative Strategy Universes, Standard & Poor's.

SUMMARY AND COMMENTS

1. Hedge funds do not defy definition, but their eclectic
nature makes them different from traditional money managers in terms of the ability to differentiate them by fixed categories of style. It is a mistake to try to homogenize hedge
funds within their asset class, or worse, in terms of other asset
classes. As will be often repeated in this book, the eclectic and
complex nature of hedge fund management reserves them as
the province for investment by sophisticated investors who
can tolerate the risk of losing their entire investments.

2. Relative Value is more of a "hedged fund" than a hedge
fund. Though never without risk, Relative Value managers
aim for rates of return generally less ambitious than those
sought by managers of the other four hedge fund strategies.

E X H I B I T   1–6

Incremental Allocations of Alternative Strategies
to International Stocks
10 Years Ending 12/31/96

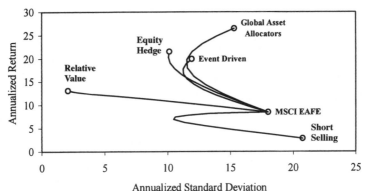

Source: EACM Alternative Strategy Universes, Morgan Stanley Capital International.

3. Equity Hedge and Global Asset Allocators are different but probably come closest to the typical image one has of "hedge funds" in terms of potentially attractive returns. Needless to say, these strategies are not without risk and some mystery in the process.

4. Event Driven encompasses a fairly straightforward set of strategies. Busted deals or misread bankruptcies can mean awful times in these shops for performance.

5. Short Selling is very defined in strategy and goal. Perceived market direction often guides the selection of this strategy, which is a leper in a bull market.

CHAPTER 2

Quantitative and Qualitative Characteristics of Specific Hedge Fund Strategies

With the macro considerations of hedge fund investing from Chapter 1 as a backdrop, this chapter takes a closer look at the individual strategies, specifically in terms of returns, correlation, and risk. Any investment decision involves an assessment of risk, yet risk is perhaps the most elusive of concepts to embrace. There are many historical and quantitative measures of risk, but they describe only the past and disregard a vast array of nonquantitative risk factors; as such, they have limited relevance for the future. In simplest form, risk is the potential for something "bad" to happen, be it litigation, the departure of a key professional, or any number of events otherwise related to liquidity, politics, publicity, or leverage. Suffice it to say that the sources of risk are many and varied, are difficult if not impossible to measure, and vary in importance over time. Nonetheless, it is important to understand the factors that comprise risk. While it is useful to recognize the close relationship that exists between volatility and return over long periods of time, keep in mind that volatility of returns can never solely define investment risk. By definition, volatility is driven by many changing factors. Risk disappears only when we correctly guess the future, and we never will get that quite right.

Further on, we examine a number of more qualitative issues related to risk. Let us first turn to a quantitative examination of the individual hedge fund strategies in a format that consists of annual returns, annual correlations with the S&P 500, monthly correlations with the market, and average performance in up and down markets.

INDIVIDUAL HEDGE FUND STRATEGIES—RETURNS, CORRELATION, RISK

Relative Value

Using trailing annual periods, Exhibit 2–1a compares the returns of Relative Value with those of the S&P 500. Relative Value seeks consistency of returns, which, as the exhibit shows, has been largely accomplished over the period observed. However, late 1993 to early 1994 was a period of great stress on U.S. interest rates and, as a result, on mortgage bonds, convertible arbitrage, and leveraged transactions in general. Relative Value strategies suffered accordingly. In some respects, 1993 to 1994 was a blessing in that this difficult period reinforced the conviction that Relative Value is not a riskless strategy.

Exhibit 2–1b clearly makes the point that Relative Value is not a strategy geared to movements of the market. In fact,

EXHIBIT   2–1

Relative Value

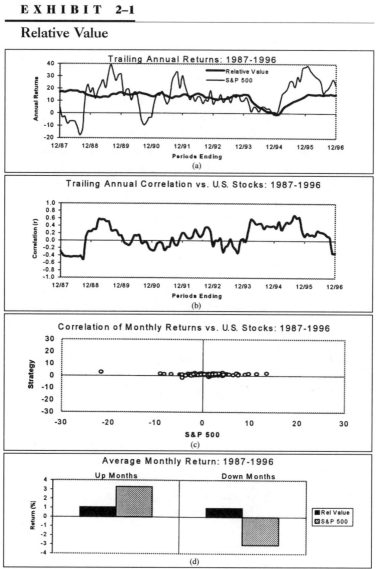

Sources: EACM Alternative Strategy Universe, Standard & Poor's.

given the constancy of Relative Value returns, the ebb and flow of correlations with the S&P 500 reflects mostly the volatility of the Index. Exhibit 2–1c shows the consistency of returns yet again; whatever the market did, Relative Value shifted minimally. To restate the point in a different format, Exhibit 2–1d shows the average performance of Relative Value in up and down markets, an indication of the strategy's potential to provide protection in declining markets.

Remember that subgroupings exist within the Relative Value and other hedge fund strategies. Though we do not repeat the above analyses here, note that, to varying degrees, the subgroupings have patterns of returns different from each strategy as a whole, as well as from traditional indices.

Event Driven

As seen in Exhibit 2–2a, Event Driven can be a creature driven at times by the market (traditional, non-event-driven portfolio managers playing deals heavily in a time of many takeovers), and at other times by a few big deals or only small deals in a market environment driven up or down by non-deal-related factors. The correlations in Exhibit 2–2b demonstrate the past cyclical independence of Event Driven from market movements. Remember that these strategies focus on a discrete event such as an announced merger or actual bankruptcy. Accordingly, the quantity of such deals in the market place governs the fortunes of these managers independent of their skills. In a period of very few mergers or acquisitions or very few distressed-company situations, returns could suffer. Keep in mind that the extraordinary returns of 1987 are unlikely to recur, since the age of hostile takeovers and their associated high spreads has given way to a more friendly sort of merger and acquisition environment characteristic of

Event Driven

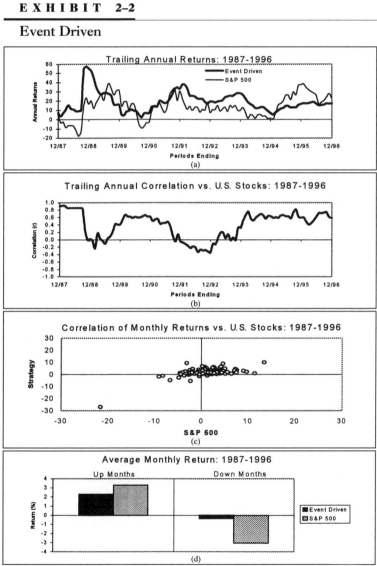

Sources: EACM Alternative Strategy Universe, Standard & Poor's.

a synergistic global economy. Note from Exhibits 2–2c and 2–2d that Event Driven strategies have neither risen nor declined at the same pace as the S&P 500 during up and down markets, respectively.

Equity Hedge

Exhibit 2–3a offers a fairly descriptive picture of the past with Equity Hedge funds. With the exception of the 1994 period (a difficult time for hedge fund strategies in general, given interest rate volatility and stress on leveraged transactions), these funds were closely linked to the S&P 500, but with less amplitude. The expectation of lower amplitude largely results from the orientation of investors in these strategies toward absolute or positive return investing. Equity Hedge funds have a predominance of high net worth individuals in their cadre of investors, and the general partner often has a significant amount of personal net worth at risk in the partnership as well. None of this precludes negative returns, but the performance of the S&P 500 up or down as a comparison is peripheral. Trying to make, and not lose, money is more important than beating an index. This factor probably accounts for much of the continuing decline in correlation of returns of Equity Hedge funds with the S&P 500 in recent years (Exhibit 2–3b). The more the stock market rises, the more defensive the general partner can become. As Exhibits 2–3c and 2–3d show, as market returns have increased, Equity Hedge returns have not kept up; nor have they fallen so dramatically in down markets.

Global Asset Allocators

As Exhibit 2–4a suggests, Global Asset Allocators are in a class by themselves. They invest across the globe, using many

EXHIBIT 2-3

Equity Hedge Funds

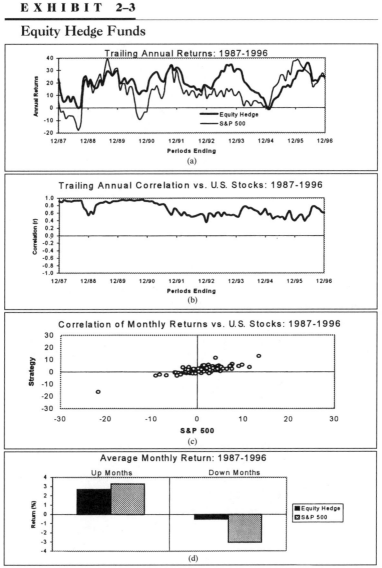

Sources: EACM Alternative Strategy Universe, Standard & Poor's.

different types of instruments from stock and bond index futures to swaps, currency forwards, options, and tangible assets. The nearly continuous lack of correlation with the S&P 500 over the entire period (Exhibit 2–4b), the most extreme among hedge fund strategies, is most impressive. From Exhibit 2–4c note that Global Asset Allocators returns were often positive when the S&P is down, and both negative and positive when the index was up.

Short Selling

One would expect Short Selling to be the mirror image of the S&P 500. When one goes up, the other goes down, and when one goes sideways so does the other. Though Exhibit 2–5a seems to support that thesis, there are lots of reasons for exceptions. For example, many short sellers short stocks smaller than those included in the S&P 500. Suppose they shorted foreign stocks, or nonstock asset classes? What if they shorted only a portion of the portfolio or even had some longs? The tendency to short non-S&P 500 type stocks accounts for most of the reduction in inverse correlation between this strategy and the index over the last few years (Exhibit 2–5b). Additionally, many survivors of short selling strategies are shorting less to stay in business. As mentioned earlier, the mutual fund-driven momentum of the bull market has driven many short sellers out of business.

Another look at the relationship between longs and shorts can be seen in Exhibit 2–5c, in which Short Selling and the S&P 500 can be both up or down together in the same month. Note also that the greater the market decline, the greater the amplification of Short Selling returns. Looking at average performance in up and down markets (Exhibit 2–5d), over the period observed, the magnitude of the average gain

Global Asset Allocators

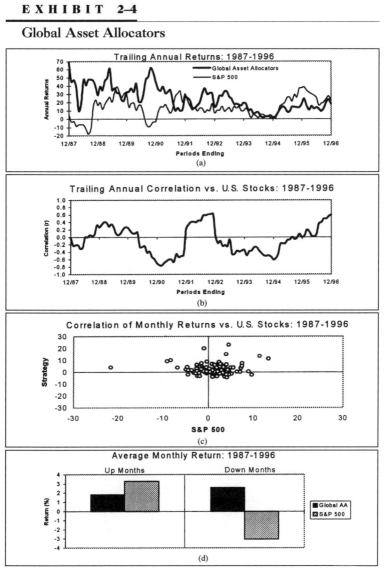

Sources: EACM Alternative Strategy Universe, Standard & Poor's.

EXHIBIT 2-5

Short Selling

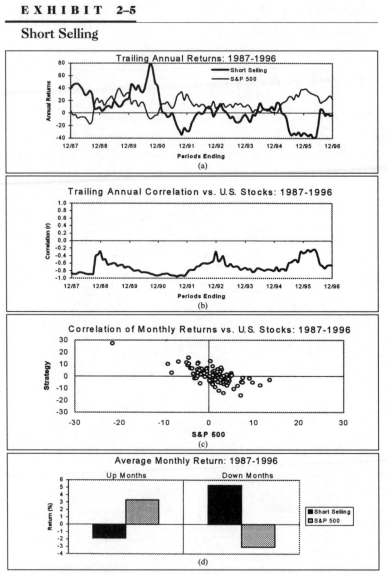

Sources: EACM Alternative Strategy Universe, Standard & Poor's.

in down markets was greater than that of the average loss in up markets.

SUMMARY MEASURES
OF PERFORMANCE

As a way of review, Exhibits 2–6 and 2–7 summarize performance of the five hedge fund strategies, in terms of trailing annual returns and cumulative returns over a 10-year period, the latter including traditional indices for comparison. Hedge fund strategies have generally been unlike one another and unlike traditional U.S. equity portfolios (which tend to correlate closely to the index). As such, they may offer diversification and risk reduction when used with traditional equity management in some proportional manner.

E X H I B I T   2–6

Alternative Strategies
Trailing Annual Returns: 10 Years Ending 12/31/96

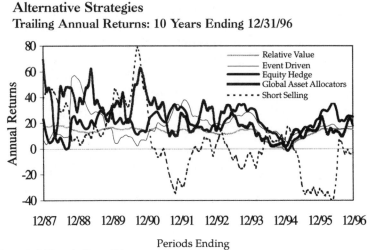

Periods Ending

Source: EACM Alternative Strategy Universes

Growth of $1 Investment
10 Years Ending 12/31/96

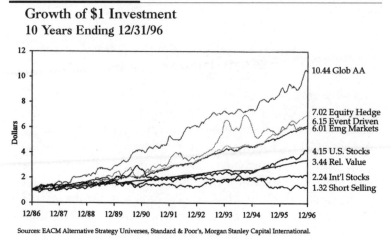

Sources: EACM Alternative Strategy Universes, Standard & Poor's, Morgan Stanley Capital International.

As we complete the quantitative discussion of hedge fund strategies, there are two caveats to keep in mind. First, the results herein are a function of the time period under observation. As Exhibits 2–8 and 2–9 clearly show, risk/return characteristics can shift when different time periods are observed. Second, the analysis to this point has focused on strategy composites or averages, which mask the characteristics of individual managers. Exhibits 2–10a through 2–10e illustrate the wide dispersion of managers around the composite risk/return characteristics for each strategy.

QUALITATIVE ASPECTS OF RISK

Up to this point, any reference to risk primarily has been in terms of some quantitative measurement such as standard deviation, which is a calculation of the degree to which a series of historical returns varies around its average return.

E X H I B I T   2–8

Risk/Return Characteristics
5 Years Ending 12/31/96

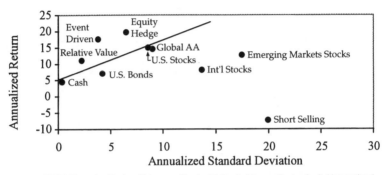

Sources: EACM Alternative Strategy Universes, Standard & Poor's, Morgan Stanley Capital International, Lehman Brothers, Merrill Lynch.

E X H I B I T   2–9

Risk/Return Characteristics
3 Years Ending 12/31/96

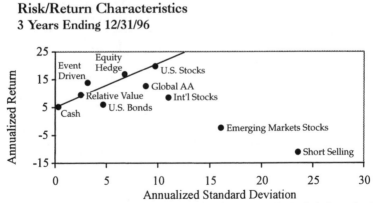

Sources: EACM Alternative Strategy Universes, Standard & Poor's, Morgan Stanley Capital International, Lehman Brothers, Merrill Lynch.

E X H I B I T   2–10a

Relative Value Universe
Historical Risk/Return Characteristics: 1992–1996

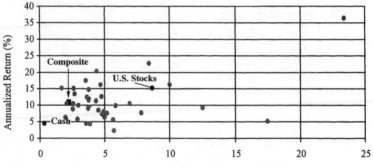

Source: EACM Alternative Strategy Universe, Standard & Poor's, Merrill Lynch.

E X H I B I T   2–10b

Event Driven Universe
Historical Risk/Return Characteristics: 1992–1996

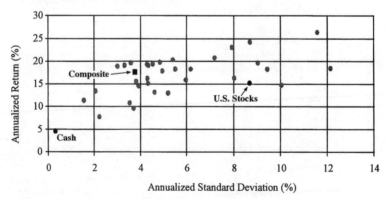

Source: EACM Alternative Strategy Universe, Standard & Poor's, Merrill Lynch.

E X H I B I T   2–10c

Equity Hedge Funds Universe
Historical Risk/Return Characteristics: 1992–1996

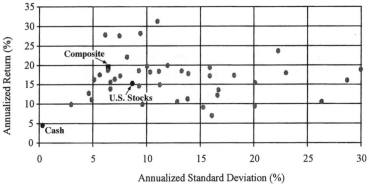

Annualized Standard Deviation (%)

Source: EACM Alternative Strategy Universe, Standard & Poor's, Merrill Lynch.

E X H I B I T   2–10d

Global Asset Allocators Universe
Historical Risk/Return Characteristics: 1992–1996

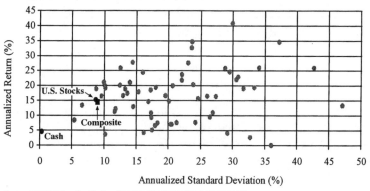

Annualized Standard Deviation (%)

Source: EACM Alternative Strategy Universe, Standard & Poor's, Merrill Lynch.

E X H I B I T   2–10e

Short Selling Universe
Historical Risk/Return Characteristics: 1992–1996

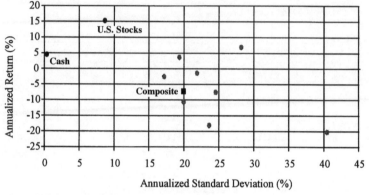

Annualized Standard Deviation (%)

Source: EACM Alternative Strategy Universe, Standard & Poor's, Merrill Lynch.

(The larger the standard deviation, the greater the volatility of returns and the higher the implied risk.) Let us now turn to a consideration of some of the other aspects of risk that influence asset classes and their selection, in general, as well as some peculiar to hedge funds.

The Human Equation

Among the relative constants that run unencumbered from traditional to alternative investing is people. We are perhaps the biggest risk factor of all, because we are chameleons, driven by emotions that are overloaded by the information age in which we live. Because of the speed of our lives, we are continuously asked to react, positively or negatively, to any number of stimuli and their possible impact on our investment course. As such, we are a risk factor, very tough to forecast, and a volatile one in the mix. In a simple sense, we all look to many varied but external investment unknowns to determine risk, when right under our hat is perhaps the most important one of all. Are we not the ultimate decision maker?

Some people insulate themselves with the cloak of a long-term investment horizon, under the rationalization that they will calmly ride out the storms by looking through them to the better days ahead. It is a great philosophy and one we support, but all sorts of doubts tend to erode our resolve: "The markets are different this time." "Our health is poor and the world looks bleak." "Our term as a fiduciary for a pension or endowment fund is ending and something bad should not happen on our watch." Cool objectivity is a rare human quality. In fact, the cloak of a long-term investment horizon is often a myth and at best porous against the storms.

Finally, some people are simply predisposed to low-risk investing while others strike a more aggressive pose. As such, some people may never invest in hedge funds. It is fascinating that many of these same people are comfortable investing in venture capital or leveraged buyouts, perhaps because the public education element of the investment industry works better for some investments and investors than others. (Chapter 8 discusses some of the positive and negative features of hedge funds versus other forms of alternative investments that can affect investor perception and decision making.) Each of us needs to bring our knowledge and experience to the decision-making table, fighting predispositions and biases as best we can. The best investment decisions are made with an open and focused mind, remembering that investing is a serious business that rewards only winners.

The Investment Itself

Any investment that has potential return also carries potential risk, some would argue proportionally so. Inherent in any investment, be it traditional or nontraditional, a directional or hedged transaction, are risks that are fundamental to the position itself.

A stock that is purchased for a portfolio carries with it the risks of market, sector, and the individual company it represents, whether it is acquired for a hedge fund or a mutual fund; similarly, a bond carries the risk of the market, maturity, issuer sector, and issuer credit regardless of the buyer. The risks go on and on, whatever the type or nomenclature of the investment and whether it is a component of a traditional or alternative type of investment portfolio. No matter who is making the decision, the questions are the same: Will the company go bankrupt? Can it make its earnings per share targets? Is management capable? Can the company pay the interest due on its bonds? Will the Federal Reserve raise interest rates?

Valuation is a factor in this equation as well, and although given to varied interpretations, it can be of great help in assessing risk levels. For example, owning the stock of a company at 4× (four times) its earnings seems less risky than one at 50×; owning a bond of a company with interest coverage of 4:1 seems less risky than at 1:1. The valuation of market sectors and markets themselves add to the complexity.

There is little agreement among investment professionals as to what constitutes high or low intrinsic investment risk. The player would say, "That's what makes markets." For the observer, investment risk seems the most fundamental of all, yet it is almost impossible to measure, much less to determine by consensus. Overlaid on intrinsic risk are many contributing factors, including those covered in this chapter. Together they are ponderable, but only marginally assessable.

Academic or quantitatively oriented observers might say that all the components of risk eventually are registered in the price action of the instrument and given enough time, high volatility probably will result in high return and vice versa. For traditional assets, they may be right, but nontraditional or alternative classes may dance to a different tune, and for many reasons reflecting both the highly eclectic nature of the various strategies as well as the combination of risk factors peculiar to hedge fund investing. As we move into that area, remember that past ratings and standard deviation are always retrospective and known while future return and risk assessment are always prospective and unknown.

We turn now, on a less than solid base, to a non-exhaustive consideration of the risk factors somewhat uniquely related to hedge funds. We say "somewhat" because most of them can be found in other environments, but rarely all together as they are in hedge funds.

Shorting

Shorting can both reduce risk and increase risk, the former as a hedging technique, and the latter as a directional bet. Actually, most hedge fund managers view shorting as a "reducer," because short positions are often used in conjunction with unrelated long positions. But even when short selling is designed to reduce risk, the result can be just the opposite. For example, convertible hedgers had a difficult year in 1994 because the bond market was weak while the

stock market was stronger. In that situation, hedged portfolios did much worse than unhedged portfolios.

The problems related to shorting are not few. In addition
to the fact that shorts can move opposite to expectations,
portfolios tend to have a long or short bias, and that bias will
often determine performance, notwithstanding the possible
benefits of an offsetting long or short effort to diminish negative returns. With the exception of Relative Value strategies
and certain other specifically designed hedged positions,
shorts are directional plays on specific companies, sectors,
or markets that the manager expects to decline.

Shorts are sneaky as well, because unlike longs, which
typically become less of a risk when they decline in value by
virtue of comprising a smaller part of the portfolio, shorts
become a greater risk. If you are short a stock and it rises in
value (goes against you), the stock becomes a larger part of
the portfolio, thereby increasing in importance and risk.

In addition, short positions are a kind of leverage,
because you need to commit no capital to do them. You simply post collateral, borrow a security, and sell it. Technically
shorting is not leverage, but it does involve borrowing, and
the possible gain is limited while the possible loss is unlimited. If the shorted security goes to zero, you are in luck. If the
security triples or quadruples in price, a potential disaster
occurs if you cannot cover the short before then.

Leverage

Leverage involves borrowing dollars to make an investment.
If you make more than your borrowing cost, it is a great trade;
if you make less, the results can be disastrous. Why? Because
your base investment cost is zero, or really negative, since
your cost of carry is embedded in the trade. As such, fully

extended, your rate of return potential is almost infinite, be it positive or negative.

As an example of the risk of leverage, let's assume you have $100 in portfolio value and borrow $100 to invest in the same holdings for a total investment of $200. If your portfolio value declines by 50%, you are broke, because the stockbroker will probably take the remaining part of your original $100 to cover your debt.

A misunderstood aspect of leverage is the ability to maintain it under adverse conditions. Stockbrokers will often lend you money to invest just as long as you maintain a value in your portfolio sufficient to cover the debt. If they feel repayment of the loan is in jeopardy, the brokers can unilaterally sell or mark down your collateral, without your approval, to ensure that they remain whole. (For this and many other reasons, the need for excellence in a hedge fund's back office and prime broker cannot be overemphasized.)

Leverage seems to make much more sense in hedged transactions, where you endeavor to make a profit from anomalies in relationships between similar securities (Relative Value). Noting that nothing these days is riskless, there was a time such transactions were possible. For example, 25 years ago you could be long IBM at let's say $100 per share on one exchange and almost simultaneously short it on another for $99⅞—obviously a trade worth leveraging and one that many brokerage firms did with great, if not immense success and, even better, with little or no capital in the process. With instantaneous information flows making transactions such as the IBM example no longer possible, you are more likely today to be long a government bond and short another of a very nearby maturity, or long an IBM convertible bond and short an appropriate amount of IBM stock utilizing borrowed funds to replicate the trade over and over again. The use of borrowed funds in investing often implies a certainty and/or confidence that cannot be ensured. Failing that, leverage serves only to magnify risk and, only potentially, return as well.

If you are a fiduciary for a tax-qualified (exempt) pension or endowment fund, you need to be sensitive to *unrelated business taxable income* (UBTI). If you are a tax-qualified fund and do not pay taxes on your investment returns, but borrow funds to enhance those returns, you may be taxed on the gains from such enhancement. Since most tax-exempt funds or organizations generally abhor tax filings, they avoid leverage either through investments they make directly or investments made in hedge fund partnerships that leverage. If the hedge fund is off-shore, where the corporate form of investment vehicle is common, a tax-qualified plan that is a stockholder of a corporation that leverages is generally not exposed to UBTI. There may be other possible tax advantaged approaches, but as a rule it suffices to consider leveraged returns as being potentially taxable to U.S. tax-qualified investors.

Leverage provides an opportunity to enhance returns from borrowed funds, but in so doing, particularly at the higher ranges, it also enhances the chance for "blow up"— that is, the chance for a "meltdown" or total loss of equity in a hedge fund. This happens periodically in the hedge fund field for a variety of reasons, but it is sufficient to say that leverage adds a great deal of rapid upward, and possible downward, pressure on returns.

People often think that by applying the usual selection criteria for traditional asset class managers to the hedge fund process, all will be well. They tend to forget leverage per se and the problems that can ensue if a general partner takes his eye off the ball. Leverage comes in many forms and, to us, is the essence of risk. Be attentive when it is part of the equation, and don't look for it only in terms of borrowed funds, but also in the forms of derivatives used.

Liquidity

Hedge funds typically allow new assets into their partnerships or other vehicles on a monthly or quarterly basis. Withdrawal may be monthly, quarterly, or semiannually, but many are annual. As a result, you are often restricted in your exit privileges to annual calendar year ends, which may or may not coincide with events in the markets, or personal circumstances that might trigger or cause a decision to change an allocation of assets to hedge funds. Upon exit, the general partner might give you a "distribution in kind"—that is, investment instruments instead of cash.

People argue that the less opportunity investors have to exit the better, because it consciously or unconsciously elongates their investment horizon. In reality, illiquidity—or expressed another way, limited exit privileges for the owner of capital—does not diminish risk; it increases it.

The General Partner

If you invest in a partnership as a limited partner, you have typically signed an agreement giving almost full authority to the general or managing partner. Though your potential liability is generally "limited" to your investment even if the partnership losses exceed equity capital, you ultimately are totally dependent on one person's judgments, work habits, health, pursuit of returns, and varying tolerance for risk. A significant difference exists between what is covered in the sales pitch and what the offering document describes—no misrepresentation necessarily intended, just materials written by different people. In sales material the general partner should tell you honestly what he plans to do. By the time the lawyers complete the documentation, the possibilities for investment strategies "may or may not" be infinite while results "might or might not" be good. In fairness to the legal profession, we have manufactured a litigious society in which to operate, and with a nod to general partners, they want as broad authority as possible in order to face the uncertainties of the future.

Remember to read all offering materials carefully (you will have to attest that you have). But when signing up for hedge fund management, expect to give the general partner full and complete discretionary control over your investment with the widest possible charter. You might do that with your surgeon before receiving the anesthetic, but can you think of many others?

Monitoring

With hedge funds little is usually known about the invested portfolio except what the general partner is willing to say on a voluntary basis. Performance results are typically transmitted to limited partners on a quarterly, or sometimes monthly basis, but audited returns are available only annually and some months after the close of the calendar year. Unfortunately, this is well past the date you would need to decide whether to "re-up" (stay invested in the partnership, a decision typically made some 30 to 90 days before calendar year end).

In the final analysis, you are heavily reliant on communications from the general partner. The cynic would say, "You are asking the mouse how your cheese is doing." A more balanced assessment is that you have picked the best hedge fund manager you can find, given him a lot of latitude, and are confident about results without oversight by investors. An exception to this is a separate account structure for your funds alone wherein the hedge fund manager has discretion to make trades but you can review the portfolio daily. (It should be noted that in a separate account your holdings need to be sizable, and meltdown risk can become a problem to the owner of the capital in that liabilities can exceed the investment.)

It is important to recognize the potential complexity of hedge fund portfolios even if you see them on a real-time basis. The general partner might think being long A and short B is a hedge while you don't. Also remember that as a limited partner, even if you receive portfolio information you have no authority to intervene. Access to the portfolio and risk monitoring, even when possible, may well not constitute risk control.

The areas covered in this chapter and others comprise some of the key factors that together constitute investment risk in hedge funds. Note that some are not unique to hedge funds and also that some are not specifically linked to the instruments in the hedge fund portfolio. The latter factors are vitally more important in almost any alternative asset class than their traditional counterparts. Such is the enigma of hedge funds in the investment world.

How does one convey a balanced, self-regulating picture of something that is inherently not? To have your money managed in a sophisticated manner by someone you feel is the "best" with all the tools and authority needed to invest, is to harness lightning. To do so requires not only informed due diligence but a leap of faith into the unknown that defines the very meaning of "high risk."

SUMMARY AND COMMENTS

1. Detailed analysis of the various hedge fund strategies further attests to the lack of homogeneity among these strategies and in comparison to traditional asset classes.

2. Some components of risk are relatively unique to hedge funds, such as shorting, leverage, liquidity, and the limited partnership structure. These often complex subjects, which require careful attention, may be relatively new areas when examined in depth by even sophisticated investors.

3. Risk is often proportional to returns, so solving the puzzle that is risk is vital in attaining desired goals. The solution is in the blending of the factors.

4. If you can get 15% annual returns from traditional equity investing, it raises the issue of whether it is worth the work of investigating the hedge fund area. Though traditional equity returns have been extraordinary for the past decade and a half, they have been less so over longer periods.

CHAPTER 3

Who Manages Hedge Funds? Who Invests in Them?

CHARACTERISTICS OF MANAGERS

The image many people have of hedge fund managers is something out of the Old West, of "gunslingers facing off" with the almost unbeatable markets. A fascination with this kind of portrait intimidates many investors into thinking that hedge fund managers have an edge that they can never have, much less understand. Whether it's guts or intellect, the stereotypical hedge fund manager always seems to be out front, charging and attacking in a business that does not tolerate failure well or give second chances. Precarious markets, either heading down or going up too long, tend to magnify this imagery.

Hedge fund managers are further regarded as rich, and in possession of some secret formula for success; those who reveal themselves in print are as exciting as we would have imagined. Rich, smart, savvy, daring, and secretive are all descriptions that together generate a perception of hedge fund managers as operating in some other world or on some other terms from the rest of us.

Hedge fund managers, on the contrary, are regular people who, like the portfolios they manage, defy generalization beyond the fact that most are college-educated males in their late 30s to mid-40s with an average of 15 to 20 years in the investment management field, half of that in the hedge fund area. Experience as a portfolio manager, analyst, director of research, or trader is an important element of the hedge fund manager's upbringing. More likely than not, experience has come from the long side of the business, meaning tradition-al portfolio management, or at an established brokerage or investment management firm. As you probe deeper into hedge fund management, you realize that good investment experience is almost always a prerequisite for success.

Suffice it to say that hedge fund managers are regular people in an albeit unusual segment of the portfolio man-agement profession. However, they do share some or all of the following differentiating characteristics or drivers.

1. Hedge fund managers have great faith in themselves and their abilities, enough to base their whole future on their personal money management skills. As one said to us, "If individual money managers think they are good, why do they work for Fidelity?" Though Fidelity is a great invest-ment house, the hedge fund mentality is, "If I am good, why water down the impact with someone else's research, com-mittees, philosophy, or process?" Hedge fund managers want to be "the best," and to do that requires ultimate self-reliance.

2. As a corollary, hedge fund managers want to control the entire process day by day. They are the ultimate entre-preneurs, simultaneously creating and implementing invest-ment strategy. Would you expect less with your own money (perhaps a big slice of personal net worth) on the line and your reputation dependent on year-to-year performance?

3. Because of extreme downside sensitivity, risk toler-ance almost never reaches the hedge fund manager's level of conviction, but that can vary with current-year performance.

In a good year in which you are playing with profits, risk can be more acceptable. Still, when your own capital and reputation are on the line with every decision, risk is not easily borne. Perhaps the greatest myth is that hedge fund managers tolerate risk better than most. Remember, high risk can mean failure or ruin and, as such, hedge fund managers constantly live in its shadow. At the same time, personal self-confidence can moderate actual portfolio risk exposure in the manager's eyes, and that factor can be a key reason for success or failure. Hedge fund managers often see themselves as risk-averse investors, hedging and moving opportunistically without regard to relative performance to indices. There is only one goal and that is to *make money*. Losing money, even giving back gains, is difficult to bear.

4. Hedge fund managers thrive on the challenge of moving opportunistically across strategies, sectors, and markets, both long and short. Boredom is almost impossible. They typically work long hours, driven almost to distraction by the need to know, because they will have to commit capital over a short horizon and it is imperative to be right. To many, investment decisions are not quite, but very nearly, a matter of life or death. For most, success or failure is always close to the bone.

5. Hedge fund managers recognize intelligence, or more specifically, dispassionate intellect combined with intuition, as a mantra. Our investment markets teach us every day that smart people are not always the most successful. One of the "legends" of the hedge fund business postulates that markets sometimes move to cadence and imperatives that are in error. To make money, you must know the truth but, if necessary, invest on "the erroneous path" to perform. That may be illogical, but such street savvy seems to give the great ones their edge. In other words, "Sometimes, don't fight the tape."

6. Though obvious from the foregoing, hedge fund managers are passionate about and consumed by what they do; they almost levitate when engaged. Managing money is rarely just a business. Moreover, hedge fund managers believe that performance results reflect them as individuals. The good ones are "killers" with an almost insane drive to succeed. For most, success is a reinforcement of self-worth, and they seek it constantly.

7. Most are in good physical condition, probably because of the stress involved and the level of intellect required. Most do not smoke, but some do. In all, they are survivors and smart enough to know that if they die, "it dies too." To compete at this level, you must be alive and functioning well.

8. We deliberately end with wealth building as a goal because it is more an outgrowth of the foregoing than vice versa. Hedge fund managers certainly think in terms of profits for their partnership, and a large proportion of that may be their own; performance fees are enticing as well. Yet many of these managers invest profits and earnings back into their own vehicles. Very few retire early, and almost all do so reluctantly. Wealth building is an important feature of operating a hedge fund, but it flows from being the best, or among the best, on roads chosen by the managers themselves. After substantial financial security is established, it becomes more a matter of keeping score of who is on the top.

In sum, hedge fund managers are reasonably normal human beings with normal failings and foibles, but driven and competitive well beyond the norm and with an enduring confidence that masks a big-time fear of failure. There is no credit for effort, just for results. It is a business in which you get used to performing, standing on a trap door, and loving and hating it at the same time.

On a personal note, we have been pleased to know many hedge fund operators, and, as with any assemblage of human beings, we like and respect some more than others. To know them is to see the manifestations of their addiction to the business. Their often aggressive, impatient nature makes a little melancholy bubble surface for those of us apprehensively concerned that their passion will consume their lives.

TYPICAL INVESTORS

Though a broad list of potential clients for hedge funds exist, the vast bulk of assets to date have been gathered from high net worth individuals, whose participation historically has reflected the individual nature of the manager and the tailored location and structure of the investment vehicle. Focused on after-tax returns, undeterred by charter or other restrictions, and perhaps desiring to be "part of the action," this latter group has been a natural investor. For many of the opposite reasons, tax-exempt institutions have lagged in their participation. The following paragraphs describe an array of investors, their current stance toward hedge fund investing, and the likelihood that allocations to hedge funds will increase in the future.

1. In addition to direct hedge fund investment by high net worth individuals, some relatively large family groups maintain a "family office" to handle investments and other family business. Most farm out hedge fund investing, but some prefer to bring professionals "in house" to manage such strategies under close supervision of the family or the family's staff.

2. Domestic pension funds, both defined benefit and defined contribution, are relatively infrequent investors in hedge funds, but in the aggregate the dollar amount can be very significant to the hedge fund area in general. The Employee Retirement Income Security Act (ERISA) of 1974 set a standard for prudent investing that underscores fiduciary caution when considering alternative investments such as hedge funds. Keep in mind that over the last 10 years, traditional equity management as represented by the S&P 500 has annually compounded at close to 15% per year. On a stand-alone basis, that is a very impressive number, not to mention a challenging hurdle for hedge funds as well.

It seems unlikely at this writing that the S&P 500 will continue at that exceptional level of return in the future, and if that is true, pension funds could turn to hedge funds for a variety of reasons, including return, possible downside defensiveness, and diversification as a function of diminished correlation of returns with the S&P 500. If that occurs, the world's largest pool of private investable assets at $6 trillion (at the time of this writing) would face an estimated current asset base in hedge funds of an incredible $300–400 billion. Even if pension funds allocated only 1% to hedge funds, or $60 billion, it would have an immense impact on the hedge fund industry.

3. Some prominent U.S. foundation and endowment funds have allocated assets to hedge funds. Much like high net worth family offices, some foundations and endowments have been long-time investors in the area, having even brought hedge fund strategies in house in an effort to both prosper and stay close to diverse markets. For the most part, however, these investors do not have a significant amount of their funds invested in the area.

4. There is little retail ("average person") investing in hedge funds, primarily because of the lack of information and experience necessary for investing in hedge funds. Further, the vehicles through which hedge funds currently are offered are not registered as public offerings, have high minimum investment requirements (typically $250,000 or more), and impose other restrictions such as a limited number of participants and minimum net worth requirements. Some retail-oriented mutual funds use concentrated positions, leverage, and shorting, but for our purposes, we would not classify them in the hedge fund category.

5. Insurance companies on an isolated basis have used hedge funds, but never as a significant portion of the General Account. This is due in part to the conservative nature of their investment programs, which reflects the fact that insurance is a regulated business subject to individual state insurance department oversight. Further, aggressive investment programs and the potential volatility of returns could affect reserve requirements and the ability to underwrite insurance itself.

6. Historically, domestic banks have tended to focus more on investing bank—as opposed to client—capital in hedge funds. Some banks are among the most sophisticated players in the field, considering for example, that banks run the primary world market for trading and making markets in currencies. In this huge spot (current) and forward (future settlement) market, banks trade *for* and *with* their customers. In effect, some banks have "hedge funds" in their structure both as profit centers for investing client assets, as well as units attentive to hedging the bank's own portfolio risks, including swap transactions for clients and sophisticated specialized product offerings of their own creation. The Swiss banks have been very active in using hedge funds for client assets, and major U.S. banks are becoming much more involved in this area.

7. Stockbrokerage firms deal actively with hedge funds in a variety of ways. They invest their own capital in both "out-house" and "in-house" funds, recommend client assets to both out- and in-house funds, and serve as landlord, custodian, record keeper, broker, and investment banker for hedge funds. They understand and are close to the business in these multiple capacities. Stockbrokerage firms also have the need to be attentive to their own "book of business," which incorporates an inventory of security and other positions needed to run their business. It is imperative to success that they understand risk exposure and manage it through hedging strategies when appropriate. In a genuine sense, these firms are themselves "hedge funds."

8. Corporations focus the bulk of their efforts on the business of their charter—medical services, steel manufacturing, and so forth. Hedge funds might be an isolated interest for some, but rarely a dedicated effort. In that context, corporations may be very active in cash management and currency hedging generated by their own businesses, but, with some exception, this is done on a defensive as opposed to profit center-oriented basis. Asset management as a profit center is not generally an internally operated part of corporate life.

9. Independent counselors and mutual funds rarely utilize hedge fund strategies for client or fund portfolios. More often the principals of these firms might consider diversifying their own programs by investing their own assets in hedge funds. However, even in those circumstances, most of their assets would be committed to traditional investment areas that they either know or are familiar with. These are sophisticated investors, but their primary orientation is away from hedge fund strategies.

10. Investment consultants and financial planners use hedge funds, some more than others. Because it is not a mainstream demand in their business, only a limited amount of time can be allotted to it. Data and manager profiles are time-consuming to generate and require updating periodically.

Still, the potential inefficiencies and opportunities in nontraditional investing motivate some firms to stay close to the area. If institutional interest in hedge funds begins to grow, these firms will have to place more resources toward the effort in order to compete.

11. *Fund of funds management* in this context is a term meaning a hedge fund constructed by investing in other hedge funds. It could take the form of a prepackaged product for smaller sophisticated investors, or for larger investors, a customized package designed to suit specific risk return preferences. Fund of fund operators offer approaches that vary from single manager funds to, as the term implies, the multiple manager variety. These funds can have a single strategy orientation, such as Event Driven, or one that combines multiple strategies seeking to represent a more diversified program. Overall, fund of funds managers can be significant players as hedge fund investors. They charge a fee for their services, usually on top of the hedge fund managers' fees. Curiously, hedge funds themselves, particularly the larger ones, are "hedge fund investors." The reasons are complex. Some have assets too great to manage internally, and they do not want to turn business away. Others believe certain types of strategies are best accessed through people they believe are experts in that area. In all, hedge fund managers are trying to deliver performance, importantly, at a cost to them that is *less* than what they charge their investors.

To relate the above discussion to the real world, Exhibit 3–1 shows the results of a survey of on-shore hedge funds in which the managers were asked to categorize the dollars invested with them in a limited number of categories. Of approximately 100 representative firms that received surveys, in excess of 50 responded with results as of June 30, 1996. Importantly, the data reflect dollar amounts, not

EXHIBIT   3-1

Source of Hedge Fund Assets

	Total	Relative Value	Event Drive	Equity Hedge	Global AA	Short Selling
High Net Worth	53%	49%	52%	70%	32%	51%
Fund of Funds, Banks, Brokers, Insurance Cos.	20%	18%	9%	19%	39%	36%
Endowments, Foundations	6%	2%	14%	7%	1%	6%
Pensions and other Qualified Plans	14%	18%	21%	3%	19%	4%
Other (including Corporate)	7%	12%	3%	2%	9%	3%
TOTAL	100%	100%	100%,	100%	100%	100%

Source: Evaluation Associates Capital Markets.

Note: Columns may not total 100% because of rounding.

investors. The High Net Worth category probably would be much larger if we were simply counting heads, as would be Foundations/Endowments relative to Pensions and Other Qualified Plans.

The dominance of High Net Worth investors and Fund of Funds, Banks, Brokers, Insurance Companies is apparent across most of the categories with Pensions and Other Qualified Plans a close third. No real surprises emerge here, except to note that Equity Hedge Funds and Short Sellers are particularly difficult areas for institutions to embrace.

Despite the current numbers, we believe more institutional assets will flow into these and other hedge fund areas in the years ahead. This survey, 5 and 10 years from now, should show marked differences from the present. If such asset flows occur, they will affect not only the size of assets managed by hedge funds but management strategies as well.

SUMMARY AND COMMENTS

1. Hedge fund managers are not businesspeople in the same sense as traditional money managers. Entrepreneurs of a unique kind, these rugged individualists often feel that what they do flourishes with them in harness, and dies when they do. Unlike their stereotype, most view wealth building as a desirable by-product of simply being "one of the best."

2. To date, the hedge fund industry has been supported and driven, not by the world's largest asset pools, but rather by high net worth individuals and a limited number of sophisticated organizations. That may change and with it may come a change in the dynamics of the industry.

CHAPTER 4

How to Invest in
Hedge Funds

The old joke from the neighborhood was: VERY CARE-
FULLY.

FEES AS A MAJOR CONSIDERATION

Though potential investors have much to consider, they must,
from the start, embrace performance fees which, if delivered,
make for a very high cost of management. The typical hedge
fund manager charges a 1% management fee plus 20% of realized and unrealized gains (total return) in a given year. Forget
for the moment that some fees are higher, and that there are
hurdle rates, high-water marks, and other items we will cover
later. Furthermore, some managers deduct both management
and performance fees from the gross return. The math speaks
for itself: If the hedge fund manager produces a 20% total return
net of expenses, 20% of 20% is 4%, which added to the 1%
becomes 5%. Not too bad, particularly when the manager does-
n't personally pay for legal, audit, and other miscellaneous fees,
and even gets indemnified. The translation into dollars is even
more awesome. With $100 million in assets under management
and a 20% return in a given year, the manager's overall fee
equals $5 million, of which the manager gets the lion's share.

For now (and it will change over time), you have to
accept the reality of hedge fund compensation and get over

it or walk away. Previous chapters have already described the depth and heterogeneity of hedge funds, yet people like to focus on performance fees as a way to define this class of investments. Performance fees, in fact, were not started by hedge funds, at least as we know them today. To take a little poetic license, pirate ships of old were a bit like today's hedge funds if you can imagine a bunch of wealthy investors outfitting a ship and sharing the spoils with the crew. In his book, *Under the Black Flag*, David Cordingly describes what might have been an outline of the first performance fee:

> A second council was then held to draw up the code of conduct for the forthcoming voyage. These articles, which everyone was bound to observe, were put in writing. Every pirate expedition, in common with most privateering expeditions, worked on the principle of "No prey, no pay." The first requirement of the articles was to determine exactly how the plunder should be divided when the pirates had captured their prey. The captain received an agreed amount for the ship, plus a proportion of the share of the cargo, usually five or six shares. The salary of the carpenter or shipwright who had mended and rigged the ship was agreed at 100 or 150 pieces of eight, and the salary of the surgeon was 200 or 250 pieces of eight. Sums were then set aside to recompense for injuries. It is interesting to observe how this early form of medical insurance determined the value of the different parts of a pirate's body. The highest payment of 600 pieces of eight was awarded for the loss of a right arm; next came the loss of a left arm at 500 pieces of eight; the right leg was worth 500 pieces of eight, but the left leg was only valued at 400 pieces of eight; the loss of an eye or a finger was rewarded with a payment of 100 pieces of eight. Once these sums had been agreed, the remainder of the plunder was divided out. The master's mate received two shares, and the rest of the crew received one share each. Any boys in the crew received half a

share. The buccaneers were insistent that no man should receive more than his fair due, and everyone had to make a solemn oath that he would not conceal and steal for himself anything in a captured ship. Anyone breaking this rule would be turned out of the company.

Perhaps there would be less grumbling by investors if hedge fund managers occasionally lost legs and arms in the pursuit of booty! Kidding aside, it is important to understand that terms and fees are only one part of the equation.

BUSINESS AND LEGAL STRUCTURES

Having characterized the typical hedge fund manager and investor, and warned you up front about the fees, we turn now to an examination of the broad context in which hedge funds operate—specifically, the variety and integration of services on which hedge funds depend as well as the regulations (or lack thereof) to which such entities are subject. To this point, we have described a great deal of heterogeneity, sophistication, and complexity across the various hedge fund strategies. The business and legal structures are no less complicated, requiring that potential investors be equally astute in their understanding and evaluation.

An authoritative review of the business and legal technicalities of hedge fund investing would be onerous and well beyond the scope of this book. The purpose of our discussion here is rather to highlight the general framework in which hedge funds form and conduct their business.

The Business Structure

Many variants of hedge fund structures exist, depending on a number of factors such as asset size, investment focus, domicile, and whether the fund is a start-up or an established entity. For illustrative purposes, let's consider a hypothetical medium-size fund that consists of an investment manager, one trader, one research analyst, a financial/operations officer, and a secretary. Exhibit 4–1 shows the structure of such a fund.

The predominant on-shore or domestic investment vehicle for hedge fund management historically has been the privately offered limited partnership that consists of a general partner (GP) and a maximum of, until recently, 100 investors or limited partners (limiteds). In general, such a structure seeks to ensure limited liability (that is, to the amount initially invested) to the limited partners. The GP typically is one or more entities granted the authority to act on behalf of a fund and to direct its affairs. If the fund is properly structured, for both the GP and the limiteds, the items of income, distributions, gains, losses, and credits are passed through to the general and limited partners and not taxed at the partnership level, thus avoiding double taxation as would be found in, for example, corporate-type structures.

Non-U.S. investors often want the services of U.S. investment managers but not the encumbrance of U.S., or perhaps other, taxation or regulation. Many hedge fund operations thus have offshore vehicles that mimic the domestic offering but are based (but not necessarily managed) outside the United States in what might be a small representative office in a tax-friendly island location; assets also are custodied offshore. The representative office keeps books and records and issues communications. In Exhibit 4–1, we show a limited liability company as the offshore structure. The limited liability company is an organizational form which, as the name implies, seeks to protect shareholders from undue liability. Variations on offshore offerings exist, but permissible tax

EXHIBIT 4-1

Operational Structure of Hypothetical Midsize Hedge Fund

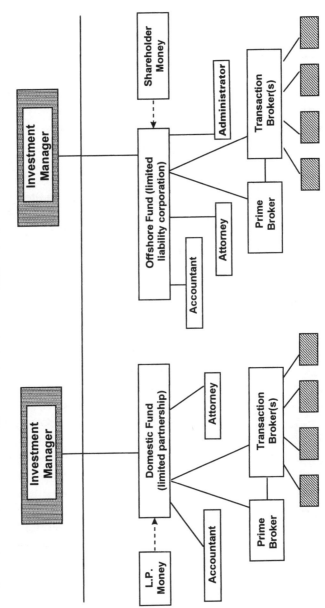

avoidance is the common goal. Notice that while the components of the domestic and offshore funds essentially are the same, the latter has an offshore administrator who acts as a record keeper at the individual stockholder level and who essentially serves as a liaison between the investment manager and the investor.

It is important to emphasize that whether the hedge fund operates in the limited partnership or the limited liability company form, investors assume a largely passive role, with little if any control over the actions taken by the investment vehicle. Investors in each jurisdiction must determine for themselves whether a particular structure works for tax and other purposes.

Our earlier discussion of leverage pointed out that offshore structures may have advantages for U.S. tax-exempt institutions that are sensitive to UBTI. If a U.S. tax-exempt institution invests conventionally in a U.S. partnership or limited liability company and that partnership or company uses leverage in the process of making profit, the institution may incur taxes on any related incremental returns. If the same tax-exempt entity invests as a stockholder in an appropriate offshore corporation, however, it may not incur the tax liability related to the use of leverage. Lest tax-exempt institutions get too excited about the advantages of offshore vehicles, keep in mind that some possible benefits from U.S. regulations may be lost when U.S. investors move offshore. Complaints about big government aside, limited recourse to U.S. regulations and laws can leave one very exposed to adverse situations. Finally, some offshore funds may prohibit U.S. investor participation altogether, while others may have shares available only at a premium. In any event, U.S. investors should comprise less than a majority of fund assets to avoid classification of the fund as a controlled foreign corporation and other reasons.

All in all, offshore funds are more complex businesses to run for domestic managers. Historical practice also indicates that offshore funds typically offer better liquidity. For domestic vehicles, investors seldom can withdraw assets more often than quarterly, and with a significant notice period; many domestic funds permit withdrawals even less frequently. In contrast, some offshore vehicles provide monthly withdrawal rights.

Accountants and attorneys are part of the hedge fund's operational structure and perform the customary functions. Given the nature of the asset class, the accounting and legal firms employed need to have considerable experience and expertise in the intricacies of hedge fund investing and operations.

The prime broker is typically the master custodian and record keeper, essentially acting as a central clearing system for all trades. (In contrast to the offshore administrator, the prime broker deals only with fund assets at the total capital level.) Short positions and margin transactions are a big business for a prime broker. Feeding into the prime broker are a number of transaction brokers that the hedge fund manager uses for researching or executing particular trades or for specialized investments. A bank, for example, might fall into this category for the execution of currency transactions.

With respect to fees, the fund usually charges a management fee and a performance fee. The management fee may vary but ranges up to several percent and is calculated against assets regardless of performance. A performance or incentive fee is typically expressed as a percentage of profits earned for a given period, and in some cases may be charged only on profits earned in excess of a specified hurdle rate (e.g., U.S. Treasury bills). In addition, certain funds provide that no performance fee will be charged until losses from a prior period are recouped.

To get a little closer to the inner workings of a hedge fund, let's assume that our hypothetical manager has $200 million in assets under management. As a credibility factor, the GP has put his own money at risk by investing $5 million in the domestic limited partnership. Importantly, note that all expenses (legal, accounting, etc.) incurred by the fund are charged to the partnership as opposed to the GP. The GP, however, normally picks up overhead (exceptions do exist) so that the fund does not pay for salaries, rent, and so forth.

The motivations for setting up a hedge fund are obvious when you consider the tremendous potential for wealth building. Suppose that our hypothetical manager, in line with many funds, charges a 1% management fee and a 20% performance fee annually. If this manager had a 15% rate of return last year, the management fee would generate $2 million in revenues and the incentive fee, $6 million. Given small staffs and the relatively few number of elements involved, it is not hard to estimate that expenses come well under the revenues to leave a hedge fund manager an extremely wealthy person (independent of the possible gains on personal invested capital).

In summary, a major characteristic of hedge fund structures is a critical dependence on one individual (the GP) who must succeed as a businessperson as well as an investor. In reality, a substantial amount of tension can exist between the GP and the limiteds. On the one hand, GPs are rarely able to manage their funds exactly as they want. Despite the stated philosophy or goals of the fund, the limiteds may too often pressure the GP to keep pace with market returns or those of other managers. The limiteds, on their part, continually have to deal with a GP who essentially makes the rules to serve partnership interests as the GP sees them, whether it be withdrawal privileges, expenses charged to the fund, or account termination procedures. Although "partners," the GP and the limiteds may have different views that often intensify during periods of poor rather than good performance and can result in an adversarial relationship.

The Legal Structure

A major difference between hedge fund and traditional asset class management has to do with regulatory requirements. Many hedge funds operate in such a way as to avoid the registration and regulatory conditions that are imposed on other types of investment vehicles such as mutual funds. Perhaps the best way to illustrate this point is to look specifically at several pieces of legislation.

The Securities Act of 1933 requires public offerings of securities to be registered as provided in the statute. Virtually all domestic hedge funds are sold through an exemption to this registration requirement for privately offered securities. Requirements for meeting this exemption include the absence of public solicitation and the meeting of certain minimum criteria with respect to the investors (e.g., net worth).

The Investment Company Act of 1940 regulates the registration of mutual funds. Up until recently, virtually all domestic hedge funds operated under an exemption to this statute which permitted private commingled investment vehicles that have 100 or fewer investors (and that satisfy certain other requirements) to operate without registering. Recent legislation, the National Securities Markets Improvement Act of 1996, amended the Investment Company Act to permit a larger number of investors without the need for registration, provided that the investors meet certain financial requirements. Note that certain tax rules exist that may make it difficult, but not necessarily prohibitive, for domestic hedge funds to actually have more than 100 investors and retain a favorable tax status.

The Investment Advisers Act of 1940 provides that managers presenting themselves to the public as investment advisers must register with the SEC. Most domestic hedge fund managers operate under an exemption to this registration requirement by limiting their client base, typically to the commingled vehicles they manage, and by not *publicly* presenting themselves as investment advisers.

Commodity laws and regulations are not applicable to managers who do not deal in commodities or futures in any way whatsoever. Those with any significant involvement, however, may be required to register as commodity pool operators and commodity trading advisers with the Commodity Futures Trading Commission (CFTC). Many hedge funds operate pursuant to an exception that lessens the applicable regulatory requirements according to certain financial tests having to do with the investor (related, for example, to net invested assets).

Most of the above regulatory provisions are intended to provide increased disclosure and protective restrictions. By "flying under the radar," hedge fund managers increase their flexibility while investors lose the intended benefit of these provisions. When investing in a hedge fund vehicle, investors typically must complete fairly extensive subscription documents certifying certain factual information for the manager's files to confirm eligibility for the exemptions noted above. Managers operating offshore and dealing exclusively with offshore investors for the most part do not have to deal with much of the foregoing.

It goes without saying that hedge funds, whether on- or offshore, need to be professionally configured by legal counsel to conform to the applicable regulations, and accordingly reviewed by potential investors. Constituent investor groups must also conform to relevant restrictions. For example, in a domestic partnership in which the GP must stay under the 100-investor limit, a single investor who comprises 10% or more of the entity can trigger a requirement that the GP count all the constituent partners within the 10% partners' group. Further, if employee benefit plans comprise 25% or more of a fund's assets, the fund becomes subject to ERISA regulations.

INVESTING IN A LIMITED PARTNERSHIP

Quite predictably, well-established general partners offer partnership participation with provisions that suit themselves and that are market driven. (For example, entry and exit privileges tend to be much more liberally accommodated in offshore offerings with general partners who also have a similar domestic vehicle.) Accordingly, investors should regard investment in the hedge fund area as a negotiated transaction: the larger the investment the more negotiable, but the more established the general partner the less negotiable.

The General Partner

Begin by noting that the general partner often requires some extraordinary advantages:

1. The general partner can accept or deny investment in the partnership or remove a limited partner as he sees fit. He pretty much has total authority over your investment during the time you are invested, and your ability to transfer your interest is highly restricted.

2. The general partner typically offers few guidelines or limitations to his investment strategy, including any related to the use of leverage. As to the latter, if a partnership uses customer leverage, the limit is 2:1 or a maximum $1 of bor-rowing for each $1 of investment; broker/dealer leverage, however, can be 10:1 or more. With futures and forwards (or other derivatives), leverage can be very high because you are settling the trade in the future and only a good-faith deposit or variation margin deposit is required to maintain the position. The question of leverage is thus worth a lot of attention.

3. The general partner typically allows himself to work part time managing the portfolio, meanwhile accepting other work and fees, sitting on the boards of portfolio companies, or otherwise focusing on things other than your portfolio.

4. The general partner may or may not invest side by side with you and probably is not required to tell you if he disinvests. The GP also may have more liberal exit privileges than you do. We remember one hedge fund whose general partner could take his share of performance fees out of the partnership annually, but limited partners' capital was locked up for three years. You will also probably never know the importance of the GP's investment to his net worth. That is, a $10 million investment by the general partner has differ-ential significance depending on whether it is 10% versus 90% of net worth.

5. Last, but certainly not least, the general partner (typ-ically using a limited liability structure itself) normally asks that the partnership indemnify it against liability if acting in good faith.

The Partnership Agreement

The partnership agreement reflects the general partner and his self-interest. Proper due diligence should lead us to focus on issues such as the following:

1. Are there any special deals for basically the same investment services? That is, are there special partners (limited or otherwise) or side letters (special deals which do not require partnership changes but give a limited or other partner a deal potentially more advantageous than yours)? Are there separate accounts with different fees, privileges, or portfolio access? Is there a hot issue account wherein certain types of limited partners (e.g., bank officers, NASD members) are not permitted to take advantage of new issue activity?

2. Are you paying any sales commissions, directly or indirectly? The latter is potentially manifested by the general partner sharing his management and performance fee with a third party for the term of your investment or for a period of years. Unless you have or are gaining a benefit from such payments, you ought to request that the fee reduction accrue to your benefit.

3. After investing, the agreement typically entitles you to access audited partnership financials. Are there periodic report letters? Presentation materials to new investors? Access to key people including auditors? Don't forget that the advantage to being a limited partner is "being limited" as to your management control, so don't get so involved as to "manage" and casually slip into the role of a general partner.

4. Limited liability is a benefit to you, so don't meddle. Invest or exit but don't involve yourself in the management of the partnership. Limited liability and restricting your investment to a modest proportion of your net worth are great risk control mechanisms in hedge fund investing.

An interesting issue is that of aging liability. Suppose, for example, that the partnership was sued in 1997 for alleged participation in events in 1995. All the limiteds of 1995, however, are now disinvested and you are a new limited partner as of 1997. Does the partnership defend itself with your dollars for events that allegedly transpired prior to your entry?

Another interesting question relates to the allocation of gains and losses and who gets the tax liability—for example, if gains are realized when you are a limited, but all the prior limiteds who were invested when the gains were accrued but not realized have exited. Many hedge funds follow a policy of allocating all realized gains to exiting limiteds, which has a positive impact on the after-tax returns of continuing limiteds. How the partnership addresses these issues, and alternative strategies that do exist, is crucial to understand.

5. Exit and entry privileges are also major items of concern. As a rule, entry is permitted on a quarterly basis (calendar year) and exit annually. (We have already mentioned that better liquidity exists offshore because competition demands it.) There are a number of good-sounding reasons for the differential in entry/exit rules, but the most obvious one is that the general partner gets paid on the basis of assets under management, so it is not in his interest to let investors exit easily. Some hedge funds are better, and a few worse in that they allow withdrawal of assets only after several years.

One of the general partner's considerations is the potential illiquidity of holdings in the portfolio (such as with private equity or debt investments), which necessitates 30/60/90 days' notice on withdrawal. Further, upon exit, the general partner can choose to distribute securities to you in lieu of cash, and you may not get the list until very late on the last day of the year. Before you get angry, remember that the general partner needs to give maximum advantage to the partnership, not necessarily to departing partners.

6. On the tax issue, it doesn't matter if you are a taxable investor or not because the general partner is, and he undoubtedly is making decisions on the taxable consequences of each transaction as well as on the investment merits. Obviously, you will have no control over booking long- or short-term gains or losses but worse is not getting the information early enough relative to year end to integrate partnership events into your total tax picture. Keep in mind that the general partner is managing the partnership tax picture and often a lot of that is done in the final quarter of the year.

7. K-1s (tax reporting documents) are worth asking about. Some general partners get them out well in advance of April 15 and some do not, in part because of the size and complexity of the portfolio and in other cases just because it is not as high a priority as it should be. If you don't like to get tax filing extensions, be sure to ask about K-1 timing.

8. It is important to understand which partnership-related expenses are paid by the general partner and which are paid by the partnership itself. How are "soft dollars" (transaction brokerage resulting in "free services" to the partnership in the form of rent, computers, research, etc.) used and for what? What is the operating expense ratio—that is, all general partner fees and partnership costs as a percentage of partnership assets?

9. As noted at the beginning of the chapter, fees are everyone's hot button and they range anywhere from 1% and 20% (1% management plus 20% of realized and unrealized total return) to 4% (or higher) and 30% (or higher). At 1% and 20%, you are paying 5% for management of the portfolio in a 20% return year; at 4% and 30%, you are paying 10%. As stated before, get used to these fee levels or avoid the area for now.

In passing, it is worth checking when the general partner is paid (in advance or arrears) and whether or not he leaves his fees in the partnership. Remember that general partner fees are so high in hedge funds that it is not necessary to be "the best" consistently to become rich by many people's standards.

Attention must be paid to a feature called a *high-water mark* or *loss carryforward*. In simple terms, you want to be sure the general partner cannot charge a performance fee if you have not made money. For example, if you lost $100 the first year and made $100 back in the second year, there should be no performance fee in the second year. However, if the partnership only had a "same-year lookback," the first year would be ignored and a performance fee paid.

Generally, a high-water mark is best. That is, if you make $100 the first year and $100 the second year, then lose $100 in the third and fourth years, you are not really even. Rather, the general partner must make back your initial $200 gain before becoming eligible again for a performance fee. This feature helps keep you focused both on the most important issue, which is gains of your capital, and then the GPs, in that order.

Although extremely rare, performance fee arrangements against a popular index are possible. More likely would be minimum investor returns (hurdle rates) before calculation of performance fees. There are also some arrangements (not recommended) where a minimum return of your principal is guaranteed to be realized at a future date. One mechanism for achieving these goals would be investing only a small proportion of the principal (say, 10% to 20%) in hedge fund activities hoping to make an attractive return, while maintaining the bulk of the capital in bonds. Guess which amount the hedge fund management fee might be charged against?

10. What happens if a general partner dies or becomes incapacitated? Some partnerships provide for dissolution, but some may not, provided that certain procedures are followed. Some even insure the general partner's life, although it is hard to see the need if the partnership dissolves when such an event occurs.

11. Knowing the auditor, counsel, and clearing broker (master record keeper) is key for obvious reasons. Bigger and well capitalized is better, with experience an important factor. You clearly wish to see the best people serving the partnership in which you are investing, but you should also be aware that each is there to make a profit and could, under certain circumstances, become an adversary. It is best to discuss these unusual possibilities as part of the due diligence process.

Needless to say there is much more to understand in a private vehicle offering (whether a limited partnership or other structure), but the above discussion should give you a sense of what is essentially more a "dictatorship" than a "partnership," benign in intent as the general partner believes or portrays it to be. Unlike pirates of old where the owners shared in the gains and losses, in this arrangement the limited partners participate fully in losses and only partially in gains and, yes, the general partner's fees are his alone. This means that the larger the partnership, the better for the general partner, and arguably less so for the limited. Investing generally gets more difficult with size of assets. To no one's great surprise, there are very, very few general partners who return assets to partners in order to maintain a more manageably sized portfolio. And, as the critic would point out, why should they? An investment in a limited partnership really allows the performance-fee-oriented general partner to take risks with your capital, which equates to "heads you both win and tails you lose."

Portraying hedge fund managers as captains of pirate ships may seem a bit heavy, but we think that the comparison helps illuminate the relative uniqueness of the venture. Remember that these "voyages" are opportunistically charted to anywhere using whatever legally acceptable devices are needed to get there and back with gains—sharks and typhoons abound. Let's highlight some of the key differences between hedge funds and traditional asset management.

HEDGE FUNDS VS. TRADITIONAL ASSET MANAGEMENT

Investment Structure

The investment structure of hedge funds gives great control to the general partner. Traditional equity management, in contrast, typically offers the individual investor greater control, access to portfolio information, regulatory protection, and liberal exit privileges.

Benchmark Orientation

Hedge funds are unique here because, for the most part, "they try to make money." In traditional management there is a veiled or an actual orientation to an index, so that if the index is down 20% and the traditional manager is down only 15%, he has done a good job. Such an explanation would not placate limited partners, who would still be upset that they had lost money, regardless of what the index had done.

Tax Sensitivity

Hedge funds are sensitive to taxes whether investors are taxable or tax-exempt. This ultimately can be good or bad for a tax-exempt investor, but it is something the general partner will focus on because he is invested in the partnership, and he is taxable. UBTI caused by leverage should be an area of concern to a tax-exempt investor, though in some cases it may not be a significant economic item. Also, be aware that the typically higher turnover in hedge fund portfolios can often result in a higher proportion of short-term gains.

Capacity Constraints

Hedge funds are largely unregulated, as a trade-off, they must accept constraints as to the extent of their marketing efforts, their communications, and so forth. Size of assets under management relative to strategy is an area of importance for both hedge fund and traditional asset managers as well as potential investors. Good judgment aside, however, dollars invested seem of little concern to most, but not all, asset managers. A cynic might say that nothing gets in the way of earning fees.

Transparency of Portfolio

Hedge funds offer very little transparency, so an investor has at best a limited view into the portfolio. Traditional asset management offers more transparency, though mutual funds actually report their portfolios only on a periodic basis. Few give the latter great concern, because mutual funds are typically not levering or shorting in the portfolios.

Risk

You have to view hedge fund investing as high risk and traditional asset management altogether as something less. With that said, you also have to recognize that in market declines, shorting can be a risk reducer that is available to the hedge fund manager and only in small measure to the others.

SUMMARY AND COMMENTS

1. In most instances, hedge fund investing involves high fees and potentially high income for the general partner, most of which flows from the performance segment (if you prosper, so does he). General partners thus have the opportunity to make significant compensation relative not only to other occupations but to other money managers as well. You must accept this fact without frustration from the start or decide not to invest.

2. Hedge funds come in complex and somewhat unusual structures that are devised at the behest of the general partner/manager. You must avail yourself of experienced legal and professional help when considering investment in hedge funds.

3. Hedge fund investing is for sophisticated investors who understand the complexity involved and can tolerate the potential losses.

CHAPTER 5

Evaluating
Hedge Funds

The evaluation of hedge fund managers and their products seeks to screen out the poor and identify the good. The first judgment is much easier than the second. To take the process a step further and identify "the best" is to identify very able practitioners among the good who are ensconced in a work and personal environment that supports their interests and efforts within a chosen strategy.

PERFORMANCE ISSUES

The evaluation process thus should be designed to eliminate the bad, then to identify the capable, and, by being particularly astute, perhaps to find the best in the process. The first step is to get a list of practitioners and their performance records. We have already warned you that complete and accurate performance data can be difficult to obtain in the hedge fund arena. Most newspapers, magazines, trade journals, and other familiar forms of media do not have access to or publish such data regularly, particularly on individual managers. Several services collect returns and sell or give them away, but you cannot assume that the numbers have been gathered, organized, and presented in an accurate and meaningful way. In any case, the managers listed may number in the thousands, so you may have to rely on such services as a starting point for sorting, analyzing, and establishing initial contacts.

Availability of Analytical Tools

The hedge fund area differs from traditional investing in many ways, including the availability of analytical tools to dissect and verify performance. In traditional portfolios, trade tickets are readily available to serve as a basis to build issue, sector, and portfolio performance results. Unless you are large enough to demand and warrant a separate hedge fund account, in which case you have access to trade tickets, you probably cannot access the manager's trading blotter. Worse, many of these funds have only annual audits, so investors have to rely on the manager (or general partner) for estimates of periodic returns throughout the year. Errors are possible, but data management and presentation can be misleading as well. Smoothing out monthly returns, for example, could suggest a very altered risk profile of a fund that made an extraordinary return in one month but nothing in the rest of the year. Remember, too, results net of fees to the investor are the most meaningful results; you may thus have to adjust gross returns yourself.

Unquoted Securities

To complicate the matter, hedge fund portfolios might hold securities that are not quoted on an exchange. The manager may rely on quotes from broker/dealers he works with, or even value the holdings himself. Because such valuations have an obvious bearing on performance, reviewing and understanding the methods used is crucial, particularly for thinly traded or specialty market instruments.

Dispersion of Returns

Within a group of managers constituting a specific strategy, it is important to observe the average return of the group versus the dispersion of individual manager returns around that average. If the "shot group" is tight, the average may be more representative than if it is not. Accordingly, understanding dispersion around averages is useful in building a general picture of the strategy under examination, as well as the managers using it. Let's examine this point in more detail.

Exhibit 5–1 compares returns of assets managed in the various hedge fund and traditional strategies relative to indices representing the U.S., international, and emerging stock markets. The exhibit offers a variety of perspectives, but first let us explain the chart.

In order to avoid extreme distortions in the results and graphic, we have removed the top and bottom 5% of performers in each universe over the period. The remaining managers are divided into four percentile ranges: 5th–25th, 25th–50th, 50th–75th, and 75th–95th. These four ranges are otherwise referred to as "quartiles" and represent the stacked boxed regions in the exhibit. The breakpoints are shown underneath for your convenience. With regard to the indices, represented by the symbols, note that the S&P 500 relates primarily to the returns for U.S. equity, and EAFE and EMF to the returns for international and emerging markets, respectively. None of the indices really relate to Relative Value, and only the S&P 500 in some measure relates to Event Driven and Equity Hedge. All the indices are relevant to Global Asset Allocators, while Short Selling relates just to the S&P 500 and then only inversely.

EXHIBIT 5-1

Alternative vs. Traditional Universes
Three Years Ending 12/31/96

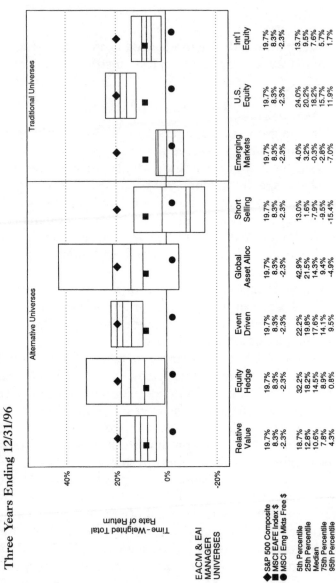

First look at the bars against one another. The larger the bar, the greater the diversity of individual manager returns within that category. During the period observed, Global Asset Allocators had the greatest variability of manager returns, but diversity within each of the other asset classes is enough to make the point that group averages alone can be misleading. It is also important to notice that, with the exception of Short Selling and emerging markets, almost all the managers, regardless of their percentile ranking, made money during the period. With the same two exceptions, the bars are really in the same "ball park." In other words, one strategy might generally be ahead of another, but at least over the period observed, they are not that far apart. That fact should raise some questions. Weren't hedge funds supposed to outperform traditional assets, such as the S&P 500? Some did, but we cannot expect the S&P 500 to achieve 19.7% per year over normal or longer periods.

Consistency of Returns

Consistency of results is another desired characteristic in trying to choose a manager. First quartile performance is preferable, but is a rarity in traditional asset management, and in nontraditional or alternative investing as well. Because the following performance comparisons may be confusing, let us first explain the format that will be applied across the strategies. Importantly, each strategy has its own respective universe for performance comparisons, so when you look at Relative Value exhibits, for example, only Relative Value managers are posted therein. Exhibit 5–2 shows the layout using the 1991–1994 period as an example, and note that each circle in Exhibits 5–3 to 5–7 represents an individual manager.

E X H I B I T   5–2

Manager Performance Comparisons

	1st quartile 1994 & 4th quartile 1991 - 1993	1st quartile 1994 & 2nd or 3rd quartile 1991 - 1993	1st quartile both periods
1 9 9 4	2nd or 3rd quartile 1994 & 4th quartile 1991 - 1993	2nd or 3rd quartile both periods	1st quartile 1991 - 1993 & 2nd or 3rd quartile 1994
	4th quartile both periods	4th quartile 1994 & 2nd or 3rd quartile 1991 - 1993	1st quartile 1991 - 1993 & 4th quartile 1994

Annualized 1991 - 1993

E X H I B I T   5–3

Relative Value

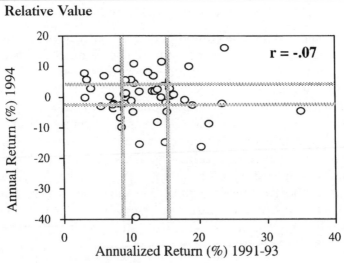

Source: EACM Alternative Strategy Universe.

E X H I B I T   5–4

Event Driven

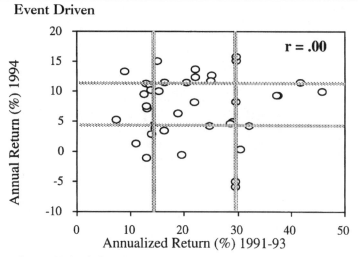

Source: EACM Alternative Strategy Universe.

E X H I B I T   5–5

Equity Hedge Funds

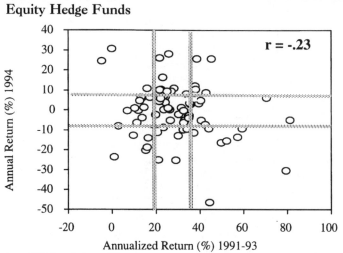

Source: EACM Alternative Strategy Universe.

E X H I B I T   5–6

Global Asset Allocators

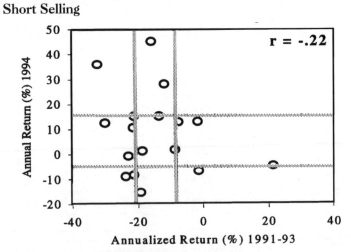

Source: EACM Alternative Strategy Universe

E X H I B I T   5–7

Short Selling

Source: EACM Alternative Strategy Universe

As you can see, with rare exception the correlation coefficient (r) has a small value, suggesting that quartile rankings of individual managers from one period to the next are independent of one another. The clustering in the middle, as opposed to the upper-right-hand box or lower-left-hand box, sends something of a message, at least when calendar year is compared against calendar year. Students of aerial combat estimate that 5% of the pilots account for 40% of the kills. That finding carries a thought we might apply to the potential for managers to attain consistent excellence, which only reinforces the importance of good manager selection.

When historical "representative performance returns" are used, particularly in an area with a growing number of practitioners such as hedge funds, two complications emerge. The first is that the sample average contains more managers in the end period than in the beginning period; the second is that the data tend to have a "survivor bias" in that the poorest-performing managers leave the database by reason of going out of business. If performance data are available for managers no longer in business, they should be included in any analysis.

Disclosure and Information

Another note on performance issues has to do with full disclosure for individual managers. Be sure that any data you examine reflect performance of all accounts or partnerships the firm manages, and be sure that you understand the firm's operating charter in order to best determine what is really representative of the firm.

Keep in mind that, with some exceptions, hedge fund managers can do limited marketing, and unlike traditional managers, they cannot or will not beat a path to your door, either actually or through advertisement. Accordingly, you will have to find them before you can evaluate them, and that takes work.

Many high net worth individuals have spread "the gospel of names" to friends and acquaintances, basking in the reflected glory of the great success stories of a manager to whom they have given assets. Other potential investors rely on stockbroker referrals of hedge fund managers whom they may know and respect. Still others use consultants or fund of fund operators to develop a prescreened universe.

Generating a Candidate List

Unless you have some inside knowledge of hedge fund managers, you need to develop some arbitrary culling techniques to reduce the number of candidates to a manageable level. For example, you might look only at managers with three-year performance records (in essence, leave the start-up firms to the pros). In the same vein, you might also require that the manager be running at least $50 million in assets.

The next step is to rank the performance of the remaining group by their particular strategy (Relative Value, Event Driven, Short Selling, Equity Hedge Fund, Global Asset Allocator) by year and, if possible, over three- and five-year periods as well. Eliminate the obvious laggards and then study the data a little more. Again within strategies, are some more volatile than others? Are some more consistent in rankings?

From this somewhat arbitrary process you will have identified a manageable number of managers to scrutinize further. It is important to note that this book is written for the beginner and not for the "pro." If you were the latter, your staff and experience might have accomplished the culling process by a means more akin to personal knowledge than mechanistic ranking. Either process nonetheless gets the number of names down to a group that permits more personal evaluation.

Regardless of the specific process, the analysis requires that you or a trusted representative gather good, solid facts about the managers under consideration. At the end of the day, the final decision depends on a subjective judgment based on "feel" and intuition. The better the groundwork, the more likely the subjective judgment will be firmly based.

As a final performance issue, remember the age-old admonition that "past performance is not necessarily indicative of future results." This has particular application to hedge funds, which are dramatically affected by one person who, over time, naturally evolves, changes, and matures. As always in the investment business, driving through the rear-view mirror can have tragic consequences.

DESCRIPTIVE INFORMATION

In gathering the relevant facts on the "short list" of candidates, it helps to develop a profile of each manager. Let's go item by item on various pieces of information to get a sense of value and importance of each.

Name

Getting the name may seem obvious, but for some frustrating reason hedge fund managers frequently do not use their own names. John Smith as general partner, for example, may not call his partnership by the name Smith & Co., but rather by the name of his street or some other not-so-obvious designation. The name of the partnership is a simple item, but associating it with the actual general partner is particularly important in discussions with others. We cannot list the times we have received calls from people who refer only to one identifying name, and it is not the name that rings the memory bell.

Location

Location is another obvious item, but in the final stages of the manager selection process, proximity or personal travel patterns may be an important consideration. Hedge fund managers tend to be concentrated in big towns, but not always. In a recent survey, we found that 44% of hedge fund managers operated from New York City and its suburbs, 5% operated from London, and 4% each from San Francisco and Chicago, with the remainder scattered across the United States and other locations.

Key Professionals

Both the identity and backgrounds of key professionals are vital pieces of information. How many years of experience does each have, with whom, doing what? What is the length of tenure with the firm under consideration, and what was the progression in responsibilities? Education is nice to know, but it is not as important as knowledge of the hedge fund product they manage. Do they invest in it, know every transaction, "breathe it"?

Assets Under Management

It helps to know the total assets managed, the vehicles and strategies offered, the number of investors and, if possible, their identities. This information can reveal a lot about capacity, orientation, and focus.

Organization/Administration

You need to understand the legal structure in which you are investing, its date of origin, and predecessor funds if any. Key investment professionals aside, is there enough staff to ensure tight controls? Is the back office sufficiently staffed and experienced? What does the ownership of the general partner look like, and what are the affiliations? Registrations such as commodity pool operator (CPO), commodity trading adviser (CTA), and broker/dealer can often reveal the depth of investment orientation toward certain instruments and possibly give you some comfort.

Who formulates policy and who does the research? The extent to which research is internally or externally generated can add or subtract from the confidence level in a firm's expertise. Ongoing litigation must also be checked, both for situations in which the firm is the initiator of the suit and situations in which the firm is the target of the suit.

Audited financials and the frequency of written reports (why not always monthly and faxed?) are vital areas. Are key managers taking new money? If not, why? Are they having trouble investing? Can you invest more money with them in the future? Will fees rise?

Investment Strategy

Understanding the investment strategy is the soul of the endeavor. Offering documents may not always articulate strategy as much as an interview might, but both sources of information can supplement and provide checks and balances against the other. Has the investment strategy been consistent over time? More specifically, has good historical performance resulted from this strategy, and if not, why?

Beyond understanding the strategy, do the approach and objectives conform with your own personal goals? Are there others using the same or a similar approach?

Portfolio Characteristics

Portfolio characteristics reflect investment strategy and thus are vital to understand. Essential questions here are whether portfolios are concentrated or diversified, global or regional, market/economic/industry sector-specific or not, directional or hedged, and fundamentally or systematically (technical/momentum) driven. Fund managers should demonstrate their approach by example, and disclose trading positions and diversification across securities, sectors, and companies. Leverage and long/short portfolio configurations can easily reach high levels of complexity, so spare no effort in understanding current and past usage; the same applies to derivatives, which come in many packages. Illiquid (private) investments affect liquidity, so probe this one deeply too. In all, specific information may be very difficult to get for a small investor, and possibly a large one as well.

How much of partnership assets is managed by "outside managers"? Does the firm use external managers for better ideas, because it lacks the capacity internally, or because it has more faith in someone else on a particular trade? Finally, the extent of stop or loss limits speaks volumes about most managers' tolerance for loss.

Product Terms

Limited partnerships and limited liability corporations are the typical offerings, but if you are big enough or powerful enough, a separate account may be possible. Negotiation of fees and terms tends to be much more of an open item with unlimited liability. In either case, is there a loss carryforward or high-water mark? (We have been over that issue.) Entry and exit obviously affect the ease with which investors can invest and access their assets.

"Management exposure" indicates the extent to which the general partner (and possibly significant others in the business) invests alongside the clients. This is significant not so much in terms of dollar amount but rather as a percentage of the general partner's net worth, a distinction worth probing.

Auditor, counsel, and clearing agent are relevant "others." Do you know them? Can they serve as a reference for the partnership?

EVALUATING SPECIFIC STRATEGIES

Gathering the information is an important first step, but what next? Clearly you need to take a closer look at investment approach, style, and philosophy. Chapter 1 identified five distinct categories of hedge funds, some with additional subcategories. Though many areas of evaluation overlap, each category nonetheless has a different focus, which requires a different set of manager skills.

Relative Value

As we explained, Relative Value is the only strategy generally focused on linking positions in a hedged fashion. Given that perfect hedging is rarely (perhaps never) possible, however, be realistic in your expectations. Above all, remember that Relative Value is a risk-averse strategy, so highly concentrated or leveraged portfolios go against the grain and should be viewed with extreme caution and skepticism.

Among the specific subgroups of Relative Value, remember that *long/short equity* managers combine long positions in stocks they think are undervalued with short positions in stocks they think are overvalued, usually balancing the two by attentiveness to markets, economic sectors, industries, capitalization sizes, and so forth. Whether driven by fundamental or quantitative methods, credible managers thus should be dyed-in-the-wool analysts with extensive experience in their specific market area. Too few issues owned, lack of organization or attention to detail, or insufficient knowledge of their area of focus all run counter to the conservative calling of the strategy.

Convertible arbitrage managers buy the convertible bond (or other convertible instrument) and then short an appropriate amount of the same company's stock to create a hedged transaction. Since this strategy tends to use a lot of leverage, the tolerance for risk is a key question here. Suffice it to say that as risk levels increase through leverage, the analysis required of the manager increases geometrically. Determining the hedge ratio between the convertible and the stock is an art form, based on factors moving the stock and bond that are away from the trade itself. Concentration is also an issue here.

Bond hedging practitioners vary somewhat, but are generally long a higher-yielding fixed income instrument and short another at a lower yield, maintaining as close to a hedged position as possible. Leverage and tolerance for risk are also big issues here. In this and the strategies above, a certain degree of street savvy is important, as is back-office strength for understanding and facilitating trades, especially the shorts. Finally, knowing the proportion of the general partner's net worth invested side by side with you can give some comfort. This is always the case with high leverage strategies.

Event Driven

Event Driven is deal arbitrage and distressed-securities investing. As mentioned earlier, deal arbitrage is one of the few hedge fund strategies with specific industry data, including number of deals, spreads, industries involved, types of transactions (stock, cash, etc.), and deals that are canceled. Investors in Event Driven hedge funds need to stay close to these data.

Quick, thorough, and competent assessment of announced deals is the key to success in deal arbitrage. Does a management firm have the staff or outside consultants to do just that? Going over prior deals, particularly the chronology, will give you insight into how key managers work; examining returns, by deal, will help you judge their competence. Do they tolerate, or even favor, deals in highly regulated industries? Do they hedge deals where possible, or are they "always certain"? How diversified are their portfolios? How have they handled broken (failed) deals? Who pulls the trigger, and where is that key player 24 hours a day? Do managers hold stock after a deal (feeling they then really know the company), or do they simply move on to the next merger or acquisition? Keep in mind that a deal arb who becomes a stock picker incorporates a greater degree of market risk than is usually present. Remember that a deal arb has some share of market risk because, in a falling market, deal factors seem to sublimate to market outlook. Do deal arbs hedge this possibility?

Because distressed-company investing tends to march to a different beat, you need to be especially attentive to the people implementing the different strategies. Generally, distressed investing involves the kind of analysis that many avoid or that is hard to develop. Although it calls for intuition or market sense, it is more fundamentally based and away from the need for strict market timing (although the timing of the reorganization can be critical). The key to the enterprise is the close analysis of asset values and bond provisions. Is the company experiencing fundamental operating problems, or is it merely a "poor company with bad capital structure"?

If the company is insolvent, are there instruments that are themselves sufficiently collateralized to be solvent, despite bankruptcy? Even in bankruptcy, will there be sufficient net worth to leave value in the stock? Should you establish a blocking (negotiating) position by gaining a controlling piece of a tranche of securities? Should you become an insider by joining the creditors' committee, thereby knowing all but being subject to trading limitations?

There is a dark side to this type of investing that requires not only a toughness of skin to endure prolonged exposure to investment situations that are confrontational by their very nature. In addition, the investor must have a great deal of confidence in his own valuation analysis. In short, it takes a special kind of analytically confident person to manage deal arbitrage and distressed-securities portfolios.

Equity Hedge

Equity Hedge fund managers, again, are those who typically started out as traditional equity stock pickers, eventually adding some short positions to reflect their opinions but also to exercise what they believed to be a market hedge.

The issues to probe here are related to stock-picking skills and downside risk. Can these managers pick stocks? What is their typical net market exposure? How diversified are their portfolios? Stock pickers tend to be poor market timers who fall in love with a company's prospects, forgetting that in a down market even the stock of good companies declines. How then do they control risk?

If you perceive analytic weakness in an Equity Hedge fund manager, run do not walk to the nearest exit. It is not unusual for a single stock holding (typically long, but possibly short) to reach 20% or more of the portfolio. The manager you are looking for is someone consumed by his companies, but able to admit a mistake and sell. That perhaps is the greatest source of strength in a portfolio manager of this kind.

Shorting, also based on stock selection, tends to be an integral part of Equity Hedge fund strategy, but a secondary consideration. The same analytic passion is typically directed at shorts, and the "need to be right" can get way ahead of making money, so probe the balance in the manager. Be wary of managers with no real experience shorting securities.

Global Asset Allocators

Global Asset Allocators almost defy evaluation in depth. Remember that they invest long or short, all over the globe, in virtually any type of investment on a levered and unlevered basis. As a result, they are opportunistically exposed to any potential gain or loss. You must therefore focus on the primary strategies and instruments employed in the near-term past and evaluate the people engaged in each respective area. Are they experienced and knowledgeable? Importantly, who determines the markets and instruments on which to focus?

In what areas has performance been most impressive and least impressive, and why?

As the big brothers of Equity Hedge fund managers, how well have they expanded their skills from stock picking to financial futures and currency trading? Have they become Global Asset Allocators as a result of philosophical choice, or by virtue of asset growth? If the latter, are they invested in things in which they have experience or even a reasonable understanding? Have they hired the right analysts, and how substantial is the analysts' input into major decisions? Global Asset Allocators are more likely than others to hire outside managers; determine how many are used and why. In sum, probe deeply to find the managers' skill sets and organizational strengths, not where they believe the world is going.

We earlier differentiated between Global Asset Allocators who are fundamentally driven versus those who are technically or momentum driven in orientation. The latter rely on systems as opposed to fundamental analysis of the investment category itself. Evaluating systems can be very difficult, especially because such managers feel their methodology is proprietary and, if they tell you, "everyone will know." They want you to understand the philosophy and not the innards, while you need more of the latter than the former. How can you bridge the gap? Focus on stop or loss limits because most of these systems are driven by market momentum (long or short), and try to find out the tolerance for volatility. Is the same system used for each asset category, or a different one for each? Fundamental analysis and technical systems are combined in many futures-oriented Global Asset Allocator strategies, and this makes the analysis all the more difficult. You must evaluate two types of systems, not knowing in advance which one will drive future strategy.

We would argue that Global Asset Allocators are the most complex managers to evaluate, so plan on a long and frustrating process. In short, do not invest if you do not understand, or plan on taking a very big leap of faith.

Shorting

As a stand-alone strategy, Short Selling requires a special breed of thinker, clearly someone looking to take advantage of unseen trouble before the rest of the world sees it. Analytically, short sellers are the classic bottom-up managers who try to know their companies inside and out and turn over every rock to find fraud or weakness—and they do so with great conviction and willingness to stand alone. Typically not heavily leveraged, short sellers face their greatest risk by falling in love with their bad companies.

At the time of this writing, the bull market rages on and short sellers are suffering. The logical person might look at poor returns and conclude that shorting is dead as a viable, stand-alone strategy. That would be a mistake, but any evaluation of a short manager in this environment must consider the personal morale and staying power of the manager. Are assets under management adequate to support the business? Might the manager chicken out and be long some stock going forward? How much capital has the manager lost in the partnership? Will key employees persevere? Is the firm changing its basic philosophy or approach to lessen risk? You may be sure that shorting will survive, but the key questions here relate more to the dedicated practitioners. Short managers believe the storm is near, almost all the time, but can they survive until the rain?

THE DECISION-MAKING PROCESS

The qualitative portion of manager evaluation is based on, but not determined by, information gathering. It is relatively easy to reach a negative judgment on a manager because of information or impressions transmitted during an interview. The manager may be evasive, for example, or may not know each instrument in the portfolio. A lack of familiarity with relevant markets or securities and an unwillingness or inability to provide data are additional reasons for caution. On the positive side, you might find that the research and decision-making process is clear and supported by many actual examples. You might also determine that both the general partner and staff are sharp, employee turnover is low, and assets under management are growing in a controlled fashion. It helps to have had experience in manager evaluation, but a serious interested person with good reasoning powers and an ability to learn can do an able job as well.

Remember, the objective of the foregoing process is to consider or "rate" each individual manager on a large number of characteristics in order to arrive at a general conclusion to hire or not to hire. Clearly, there are more characteristics and possible outcomes than can be dealt with here. As the above examples demonstrate, "good" and "bad" are often relative terms that depend on the situation and strategy. Further, you may react differently to similar answers on identical questions from different managers. Even so, once you arrive at a set of evaluations with which you are comfortable, you will rarely find that a manager falls entirely on the negative or positive side, thus simplifying your decision. To reach the final outcome, a couple of rules apply:

Rule 1: A single negative factor can dictate the decision not to hire a manager, but no single positive factor can drive a hiring decision. Investing little personal capital in the partnership, serious illness of the portfolio manager or close family member, dissolution of the firm, a significant regulatory problem, a lack of cooperation with regard to monitoring requirements—each is a reason on its own for not hiring (or for firing) a manager. On the other hand, even top decile performance in each of the last 10 years singularly does not guarantee or justify a hiring decision.

Rule 2: Managers with a preponderance of positive characteristics generally are candidates for hire, whereas those with a majority of negative concerns are not. Moreover, comparisons with a competitor's positive and negative characteristics also are worth considering. A well-respected organization with experienced professionals and a good performance record, for example, also may be experiencing a too rapid growth in assets appropriate for its style or professional staff. All other things being equal, a manager without this concern is the safer hire.

Some people shortcut the initial research and screening process by simply following recommendations of their friends. As such, they enter into interviews ill prepared for the process. This approach is unrewarding, and ultimately costly.

The hedge fund evaluation process rarely wind ups in a "beauty show" format: the relatively comfortable scenario of five finalists presenting to you or your committee on a single-day, back-to-back basis. Preceded by the necessary research, that venue can provide a comparative forum that facilitates decisiveness. The comparison more often is done on the fly from one manager to another by people who must stay sharp and focused.

Whatever the approach, you will still have a sense of being checked out during the interviews. It is similar to attempting to join a club whose members screen their prospects while they themselves are being placed under the microscope. In other words, "They are doing you while you are doing them."

It is difficult if not impossible to identify the best, or even the best for you. You can, however, isolate those whom you believe to be "good." We argue that the process is so risk prone that no one should hire one hedge fund but, rather, multiple managers to do the job desired. Surely it provides diversification but also takes a great deal of pressure out of the evaluation and selection process. In essence, the multiple-manager orientation flows from the nature of the beast. The investor in hedge funds seeks high "manager-specific alpha" and is willing to accept high "manager-specific risk": that risk can be diversified and, we believe, should be diversified. If you are a purist and seek perfection, it is easier to identify "the best" from a multiple-manager array and real experience, basing your judgments on a live, intimate relationship, rather than on a beauty show that goes from "20 prospects to picking only one."

As a final note, etiquette and common sense always require that the winners and losers be notified as soon as possible to advise them of the results and, if appropriate, to provide them with an explanation for the outcome. The managers deserve this courtesy given the time and expense committed to the presentation and their heightened expectations. It also goes without saying that preservation of a good relationship for the possibility of future business is important.

Bear in mind that prior to selecting a hedge fund manager, you have already made some major decisions that themselves will have a major impact on your portfolio, including the decision to move money from traditional assets to hedge funds, and the amount, the asset strategy itself, and the monitoring that follows. Although the selection of managers is very important, you get more than part way home before you get there, and individual manager analysis takes it even closer. From that perspective, manager selection is not an all-or-none decision.

SUMMARY AND COMMENTS

1. The foregoing quantitative and qualitative criteria for evaluating hedge fund managers serve only to convey a sense of the process. In fact, no precise formula exists to ensure the identification of managers who consistently will meet their goals and outperform all others in their category, no matter what the asset class.

2. Hedge funds are not homogeneous. In fact, differences exist not only among the five strategy groupings but within them as well. You must understand the potential for each strategy and how well that fits your goals. In evaluating managers, you must first know the strategy and then analyze managers within it.

3. Evaluation involves fact gathering followed by analysis. Fact gathering starts with performance screening followed by a profiling of qualitatively specific investment and organizational data on the managers who pass the initial screens. In the final analysis, qualitative evaluation is more important than performance. Neither guarantees success, but the first provides much more insight than the second.

4. Analyzing hedge fund performance requires diligence and understanding. "Average manager performance" is a far more representative concept in traditional equity management than in hedge funds. Dispersion typically is greater among hedge fund managers, an area more highly dependent on manager skill than market action. Manager selection, and diversification across managers, is thus very important.

5. Hedge fund managers may not be particularly accommodating, because marketing their services (particularly for the larger, more successful funds) is not something they regard as a great use of their time. As such, they screen inquiries in order to be selective in their response, much preferring simply to "take orders" than to pitch their services. Be prepared for the reality that you either "buy their reputation" or not buy them at all. We suggest the latter, unless they are willing to give you the understanding necessary to make an informed decision. In general, however, hedge funds are small organizations, so you get the best, or worst, of one or two people in the management of the fund. The small ones tend to be more open and accepting of prospects.

6. No guide exists that specifies when to hire or not to hire a manager. Arguably, hedge funds are the ultimate money management art form and that makes the application of science difficult, if not impossible. The key is gathering significant information about managers. If they will not provide it, exclude them from further consideration. If they will, immerse yourself in analysis to reach an informed judgment. If you do not understand the information or cannot analyze it, do not invest, or invest only with a solid understanding of the potential consequences.

CHAPTER 6

Monitoring
Hedge Funds

After reading the foregoing chapters, you might argue that monitoring hedge fund investments is a fruitless endeavor because the general partners probably will not tell you too much and, further, your assets are locked up for as much as a year anyway. More than a little truth exists in these views, but there are other issues to consider, including the underlying justification for monitoring:

♦ The hiring of an investment manager involves a delegation of authority which, consistent with human affairs, requires ongoing legitimization.

♦ Monitoring enhances accountability, which is an element of the responsibility we must assume for wealth management and financial well-being.

♦ Monitoring keeps the individual or plan sponsor knowledgeably close to the increasingly complex task of managing assets in a global environment.

♦ Monitoring serves as a form of risk management.

♦ The monitoring process reaffirms not only manager selection, but the individual's or fund sponsor's goals and guidelines.

Let's also be honest about attempts at monitoring managers. Though some general partners are a little nasty or nutty, and many have egos that you'd have trouble getting into a moving van, for the most part they are reasonably affable people. If you work at the monitoring process, even make it a condition for investment in the partnership (as it should be, as part of manager selection), you will find that some "tough nuts" can be cracked. The truth is that many general partners welcome communication, particularly if you are not the press, or trying to piggyback on ideas for yourself or for friends. In fact, if you are an intelligent person and do not call too often, the general partner probably would enjoy the conversation.

Here are a few ground rules to keep in mind:

+ Reception is better during good performance periods, but a noncritical call in a bad period can also be welcome.
+ Don't call more than once a month (under ordinary conditions) and keep it focused and relatively brief.
+ Be willing to talk to lower ranks but always try to get to the "big cheese."
+ In the absence of being able to get major positions by name, stick to general areas such as whether key managers like the dollar or whether they are making money by stock picking and, if so, where.
+ In general, short positions by name are often a closely guarded secret. Wall Street would like nothing better than to "squeeze the short" by buying the stock until the general partner is forced to buy in to cover his short positions.
+ Your goal is to understand the general partner's strategy and, if possible, to disaggregate performance in a manner that lets you know how it came

about. With work, you can collect significant information toward this end.

LIMITED PARTNER VS. SEPARATE ACCOUNT HOLDER

As a limited partner of a partnership, you really have only a few levers to pull to maximize access to the portfolio. If you are large enough or important enough to warrant a separate account, however, the monitoring world changes. When you are a separate account holder, the ownership of the account is yours, and even though you may give discretion to the individual who is also general partner of a limited partnership, you are entitled to see all transactions. You can thus see the portfolio at least daily.

Though having a separate account may reduce your idea of risk, it increases risk as well. For example, if the portfolio has used leverage through borrowing or derivatives, your potential loss liability is limited not to the size of the separate account but to whatever liability the account generates. For example, if the general partner leverages your $100 by borrowing another $100, and by some unfortunate fate loses the $200, you are also liable for the additional $100 the GP borrowed. (As a limited partner of a partnership, you would generally not be.) As big a problem, however, is how to assess the risk in a portfolio that is possibly long and short, hedged and unhedged, leveraged or not, domestic and/or foreign, and so forth. In short, knowing "what you own" is no easy matter.

MONITORING RISK

Risk monitoring systems exist, and they can help a lot, but for the moment let's focus on the art form. That is, even if you see the picture, how do you make sense of what is in the artist's head without talking to him every day? A Relative Value manager may send a daily portfolio containing 600 individual positions, and you would be faced with the task of determining which positions hedged significant others. The point to be made is that the simple knowledge of positions may not render the clarity you seek, and you must not expose yourself to open liability if you are not prepared to deal with the consequences.

A risk monitoring system (if you have one) is best if it is real time, or at least daily, in terms of compilation and reporting. Equally important, its capacity must be sufficient to give you at least summary risk insights that are real. Further, the system should be totally independent of manager inputs but sufficiently in tune with the manager's portfolio construct as to avoid a daily fist fight over whether the long Dutch stock position is really hedged by the short Deutschemark position. In other words, the ideal monitoring system is independent in every way, but aware of the manager's logic.

Practically speaking, real-time risk *control* is difficult to achieve; simple, informative risk monitoring is the more realistic goal. With some work, you can put together some pieces of the risk puzzle, but not all. In the final analysis, as an investor, you should develop, or obtain your own risk-monitoring system and thereafter communicate with the manager as necessary.

Components of Risk

Risk monitoring means not just knowing the content of the portfolio, but also arranging the components in categories that facilitate meaningful analysis and insight. There are certain top-line items that are important to know. These include the amount of leverage, the use and type of derivatives, the long/short ratio and its underlying structure (for example, whether shorts and longs are in same industry), the breakdown between public and private securities, who or what service is pricing each, the degree of concentration, and the countries and currencies represented. Overall, a risk monitoring system should provide a timely understanding of the portfolio's risk/return characteristics, their consistency with the manager's stated objectives, and finally insight into the success of any multiple-manager strategy employed to provide diversification and return on a total portfolio basis.

Timeliness and Sources of Trades

Let's stay on the subject a little bit longer to address two important monitoring issues: timeliness and sources of trades and pricing. Real time means that a trade is entered into the risk monitoring system as it occurs. If you have continuous access to the portfolio structure, then you wrestle only with the judgment factor—that is, whether the impact of that trade on the risk/return profile of the portfolio is good or bad. If you see the trade or portfolio at the end of the day or the following morning, your monitoring is lessened, as is any possible control. Weekly, monthly, or longer lags in observation diminish insight and control considerably. Unlike traditional asset classes, in which people think in terms of quarterly or at most monthly monitoring, the hedge fund asset class is a creature potentially far more sensitive to market and other investment-related factors than most realize. You must keep hedge funds as close to you as possible, certainly much closer than traditional asset classes.

Where the trade data come from and who prices the holdings also require attention. Ideally, a broker provides the trade information directly to your risk monitoring system or vendor, and the public markets price the holdings. Remember, many managers will not grant access to the portfolios; others will do so only in a manner easy for them or on a summary top-line basis. Accordingly, you may have to accept the fact that some of your managers will give you nothing while others, in lieu of the actual portfolio, will provide summary monitoring reports for you. Further, some or all may actually price holdings themselves, at times with a significant difference from the public markets. As with many things in life, what you want and what you get are often two different things, but as a rule something is better than nothing.

There is an important trade-off between portfolio transparency and manager size and "status." Investing as a limited partner in a risky asset class requires that you monitor the managers closely, but some will not let you and others will provide only general information, not to mention your need to deal with timeliness and accuracy issues. Unfortunately, that's the deal, and to add to the frustration, the larger, more well-established and well-known managers with superior long-term records may be the most difficult to deal with on risk monitoring issues. So if you really want risk monitoring insight, you probably will be driven to the lesser known and less established managers with shorter records. A compromise is the most probable outcome, with a mix of managers offering widely varying levels of transparency. In any case, it is unlikely that you will consider and evaluate only managers who facilitate risk monitoring, but in a perfect world that's exactly what you would like to do.

STAYING CLOSE TO MANAGERS AND MARKETS

Whether you monitor managers by telephone, office visits, lunches, or a formal risk monitoring system, you must stay close to the happenings in public markets around the world, as well as to your managers. Depending on the hedge fund strategies that your managers utilize, some indices will be more relevant than others, but macro barometers are independently essential. For example, you need to know what is going on in the U.S., German, and Japanese markets all the time; if you have a manager investing in Spanish securities, then Spain is important as well. In short, the process of monitoring in general and risk monitoring in particular is multidimensional and continuous. This means you must strive to understand not only different trades or strategies but the whole spectrum of economic and political events around the world. Most people can get very lazy about staying engaged, or overwhelmed by the prospect of monitoring so many different markets. You might ask why the general partner, as the expert, cannot assume full responsibility for monitoring. The bottom line is that the hedge fund investor must be an *informed* investor. All in all, it takes very little effort to stay abreast of domestic and foreign equity and bond markets. Information and indices abound in the daily press, in on-line services, and in other regular forms of media. Suffice it to say, monitoring of world markets is an everyday effort, so fight the feeling to let it ride even for a day.

COMPARISONS TO PEER GROUP

Hedge fund monitoring requires attentiveness to index movements to be sure, but you also need to know how well your manager is doing relative to a peer group. The next chapter will discuss in detail the EACM 100 Index that our firm uses for comparison purposes. Exhibit 6–1 shows performance of the various hedge fund strategies for December 1996 and for 1996 year to date (Appendix II provides updated data for

E X H I B I T 6-1

Composite Performance (%)

	December	Year 1996
EACM 100™ INDEX	1.5	17.3
Relative Value		
Long/short equity	1.0	14.6
Convertible hedge	1.2	13.7
Bond hedge	0.0	13.0
Multistrategy	1.2	15.7
	1.6	16.0
Event-Driven		
Deal arbitrage	1.4	15.7
Bankruptcy/distressed	1.2	15.2
Multistrategy	1.5	14.0
	1.6	18.0
Equity Hedge		
Domestic long biased	2.4	22.6
Domestic opportunistic	2.3	24.4
Global/international	3.2	20.6
	1.6	22.5
Global Asset Allocators		
Discretionary	0.1	20.4
Systematic	0.9	23.7
	-0.7	16.8
Short Selling	5.9	-10.6
S&P 500 Composite	-2.0	22.9

Year 1996 axis: -20 -16 -12 -8 -4 0 4 8 12 16 20 24 28

The above indices are equally-weighted composites of unaudited performance information provided by certain investment managers chosen by Evaluation Associates Capital Markets, Inc. ("EACM") pursuant to guidelines established by it (which may be amended from time to time in EACM's sole discretion). The underlying performance data is net of managers' stated fees, and reflects the performance of investment vehicle(s) represented by the investment managers to be representative of all accounts managed pursuant to a designated investment strategy. All such performance data and representations are not independently verified or approved by EACM, and EACM makes no representations as to their accuracy. EACM does not undertake to correct or to update this information in any way. Past performance is not necessarily indicative of future results. These indices are intended for informational purposes only, and do not constitute advice or an offer, solicitation, or endorsement with respect to any investment strategy or vehicle.

1997). Exhibit 6–2 focuses on the 1996 monthly returns for one of the strategies: Short Selling. These charts can give you some sense of where your investments stand with respect to both strategy selection itself and the relative ranking of your managers within the relevant strategy.

To summarize, you need to get as much information from your manager as possible, using whatever means are at your command—be it cajoling, begging, early morning calls, lunches, or a separate account. Concurrently, you need to keep yourself reasonably up to speed on what is happening in the investing spheres frequented by your managers and beyond in order to better understand and evaluate the information the managers give you. The information gathering process occurs in both public and private domains, the former through newspapers, magazines, and stockbrokers'

EXHIBIT 6–2

EACM 100ˢᴹ—Short Selling

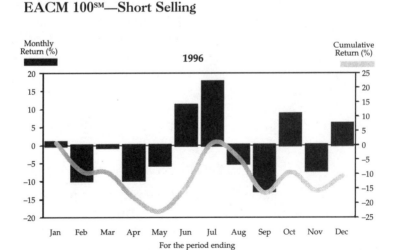

research reports to name a few, and the latter by conversations with respected sources of information such as other managers, stockbrokers, economists, and specialists of other kinds.

REEVALUATING YOUR INVESTMENT MANAGER

As the monitoring process proceeds, you naturally will reassess your confidence level in the manager—whether it is rising, falling, or staying the same. Combine that level of confidence with some comparisons of performance, starting with the manager's stated (and we presume your expected) goals, and then with domestic and non-U.S. indices to gain some sense of what more traditional asset classes are doing. Finally, make comparisons with available indices and universes of specific hedge fund managers' strategies that can serve as a peer group.

The monitoring process is an ongoing hire/fire decision. Risky and sometimes esoteric investments, high fees, carte blanche on the part of the general partner, and one-year lock-up periods are not exactly ingredients for being a patient investor. Remember that a hedge fund manager can become rich (independently wealthy) with only one year's great performance. If a poor year follows, the manager can crank up the high-water mark or lookback, but not return the prior year's fees. It is your job to be a tough, informed buyer at all times. Caveat emptor has never had more meaning.

Time Horizon

A common question is how much time you give a hedge fund manager to demonstrate credible performance. The answer is tough to generalize, but assume that the time period is shorter than for traditional areas of investment. If you have a good understanding of what is going on inside the partnership, you can allow more time than if you do not. Essentially, the decision to stay with a manager is a year-to-year judgment, based on the knowledge that hedge fund managers are selling investment management of a certain highly charged kind.

Most hedge fund managers are smart, decent folks and also good businesspeople. Some are particularly charming; some a little kooky. Many possess the allure of "a brilliant eccentric, a little on the wild side." Others are big, famous, and sophisticated, and capable of impressing you with their friends in high places and making you believe that you are lucky to be investing with them. It is not always easy to maintain your objectivity with such personalities, but you must.

Withdrawing Assets

The termination process with partnerships is different from the process with other investment positions. Many managers require a statement 30 to 90 days prior to the end of the calendar year, quarter, or month that indicates your intentions to exit from the partnership. In other words, you must decide whether you want to be in the partnership on January 1 without knowing October, November, or December performance. It gets even trickier. Let's suppose that you are terminating. In January you typically get upwards of 85% of the market value of your investment as of December 31. The remainder is usually held in money market-type investments until the audit is completed and is then sent to you. (Keep in mind that audit and other tax-related reports can be quick or delayed because of various events or circumstances.)

Sometimes the general partner will give you securities instead of cash. For tax purposes, he may want to pass on securities with embedded accrued gains to be sold outside the partnership. It could also be that the securities are more or less illiquid, and the GP does not wish to attempt the sale of such securities so he gives them to you to sell after January 1. Certain funds may also impose redemption fees.

In any case, when you exit from a partnership, you must abide by the stated partnership terms and otherwise subject yourself to the mercy of the general partner. To paint this in the proper light, the general partner could have a big problem if there are heavy termination requests, because his obligation is to protect the continuing partners. If the GP is lucky enough to have new investors coming in at the same time, only a few terminations, or a highly liquid portfolio, withdrawals are easy to deal with. To the extent that heavy withdrawals almost always coincide with poor performance or other bad news, however, the best of circumstances for the exiting limited partners are not always likely to occur.

Hedge fund managers are generally no different from other good businesspeople. If you treat them fairly, they will typically reciprocate. An inappropriate move on the buyer's side is to submit a termination notice on time, and then withdraw it on December 31. You may attempt to do so to give yourself total flexibility, but some general partners will still honor the withdrawal (pay you off) even if you cancel at the last minute. Given that the general partner requires such advance notice for termination, it may not be reasonable to expect you to anticipate your financial status two or three months ahead. In certain instances, people file a termination notice but discuss their personal circumstances with the general partner in order to work out a solution. Many general partners of individual partnerships will work with you if you are open and honest with them, though no guarantee exists that a withdrawal notice will be reversed.

For separate account holders, the termination process is similar to that of a separate account in a traditional asset class in that a telephone call can request that trading cease. The determination of who should liquidate the portfolio, however, requires a little more thought. Should the general partner liquidate the securities, since he is closest to them? Unless you are liquidating only a portion of your investment, it is best not to let the general partner liquidate the holdings, because he has almost certainly lost any sense of vested interest in your well-being. Alternatively, you could seek bids from third-party brokerage firms. Perhaps the best solution would be to transfer ownership to a new manager with a set period over which the securities could be sold in an unhurried, best-price manner. The process is quite manageable but worthy of close attention in order to shut down the account in a way that harms you least.

In closing, we should note that some investors seek intensive monitoring in order to piggyback on general partners' trades. To do so is wrong without the general partners' knowledge, and in most cases just plain wrong on its own merits. Such actions speak poorly for the investor and can be harmful to the other limited partners.

A final thought pertains to fund of funds operators and consultants, and their relative abilities vis-à-vis the monitoring process. As with any group of practitioners, good and bad are present in the crowd such that due diligence in their selection is equally important to individual manager selection. By and large, fund of funds operators are closer to hedge funds than individual investors and more often hooked into the internal professional network of both personal and investment scuttlebutt. If you are wondering whether the use of a fund of funds operator excuses investors from monitoring their hedge fund investments, the answer is emphatically no. You will need to do serious due diligence to appropriately select a fund of funds operator. You also still need to stay current on peer group comparisons and, most particularly, the investment opportunities that ebb and flow within the hedge fund spectrum of interest around the world. Whatever analysis, information, and questioning you can use to challenge your fund of funds operator can serve to enhance the practitioner's insight into individual managers, portfolio strategies, and performance attribution. Nonetheless, for investors who want to do limited work on the investment monitoring of hedge funds, the fund of funds operator can be a worthwhile crutch.

SUMMARY AND COMMENTS

1. Monitoring is often viewed as the least exciting of exercises, and that is certainly a mistake. Investing may not be your career, but it can be an important determinant of financial security.

2. With hedge funds you are almost totally dependent on the general partner, so select them well, but monitor them better. This process builds or destroys trust. Always suspect someone who tells you nothing, even with a good record; do not always favor someone who tells you all, good record or not.

3. Risk monitoring (as opposed to risk "control") systems are as close as you can get to good monitoring. It takes systems, speed, understanding, and still some trust of the general partner. Perfect monitoring, like perfect control, is a myth.

4. Monitoring requires performance comparisons with goals, indices, and peers, but it presumes that you understand more than the numbers. Performance attribution is an essential part of the process. A manager we know was up 80% in one month, and 37% for the year, all because of the colossal performance of one security. You may have signed on for that ride, but either way it is critical that you know about it.

5. There are no strict rules for firing a manager. It is simply a constant process of collecting and understanding facts that are placed on a balancing scale every day and that, for the record, are rarely neutral.

6. Hedge funds are not for investors who want performance and no hassle. No matter how gifted a general partner is, circumstances change (investment style, asset growth, change in staff and responsibilities, age and maturation). All warrant constant evaluation for their impact on the bottom line.

CHAPTER 7

Hedge Fund
Benchmarks

THE INDEXATION PHENOMENON

Indexation first attracted institutional attention about 25 years ago, after the 1960s entrenched indices like the S&P 500 at the base of our investment psyche. The hypothesis that actively managed funds, particularly those focused on U.S. equity, will underperform an index, at least in part because of management fees, expenses, and transaction costs, seems reasonable in light of most performance records. Accordingly, institutions as well as retail investors have begun to increase their use of index funds.

Regarding the U.S. equity market, another phenomenon has accounted for the rise in the use of index funds. On an annually compounded basis, the S&P 500 has gained about 11% per year, on average, over most rolling periods going back 40 to 60 years. Over shorter time periods ending in 1996, however, the numbers are closer to the mid- to high teens. In other words, "simply" buying a fully invested index not only beat most active managers and cost less on a relative basis in fees and expenses, but it also got you good returns. A decent economic environment accompanied by huge marketing efforts by mutual funds and stockbrokers has served only to enhance the immense feeling of investment well-being you had in the first place.

Indexation seems to be the clear winner in a bull market, but what about a bear market? It is difficult to answer that question, because we have not had a genuine bear market since 1973–1974. Some people even say that we have learned to better manage economic/business cycles and possibly market cycles too. If that is right, indexation is a clear winner, because stock market declines probably can be managed to 10% or less. But is the S&P 500 everything it should be for indexation purposes?

The S&P 500 as an Index

Before jumping to any conclusion, let's examine the S&P 500 as an index (using year end 1996 data for consistency). First and foremost, the index is capitalization weighted (stock price times shares outstanding), which places great emphasis on the size of companies in the market and therefore in the index. For example, at the time of this writing the top five companies in the index, and their proportions therein, are:

GE	2.9%
Coca Cola	2.3%
Exxon	2.2%
Intel	1.9%
Microsoft	1.8%

To add perspective on the size of some of these companies, GE's capitalization alone is equivalent to nearly 20% of the entire emerging market universe of countries, or the sum of those of the following companies: American Express, Citicorp, Atlantic Richfield, Aluminum Company of America, Dow Chemical, International Paper, JC Penney, Avon Products, and Digital Equipment. Coca Cola's capitalization equals the sum of those of the 28 companies in the index classified as members of the iron/steel, aluminum, and paper/forest products industries. In non-S&P 500 terms, note that Intel and Microsoft are together 13% of the NASDAQ composite.

By economic sectors, the S&P 500 breaks down as follows:

Economic Sector	Percent
Financial	15
Utilities	10
Energy	9
Basic industry	6
Industrial/multiindustrial	12
Consumer cyclical	13
Consumer noncyclical	21
Technology	14
Total	100%

Though it is tough to agree on what companies fit into differing versions of these categories, we could legitimately argue that the S&P 500 breakdown is probably not an exact reflection of the U.S. economy.

Our standard methodology is to organize data into different categories of analysis and portray the results by quintiles. Let's look at market capitalization for the S&P 500 in this format:

	Quintiles by Market Cap ($mil)	Percent
1(highest)	greater than $13,152	64
2	from $6,600 to $13,152	18
3	from $3,848 to $6,600	10
4	from $2,139 to $3,848	6
5(lowest)	less than $2,139	2
		100%

This breakdown speaks for itself in terms of biases inherent in the index. These biases may be acceptable but cause the index to lose its universal character.

Limitation of Indices and Their Use

Since market relative performance began to hit stride in the late 1960s, many indices have taken on a godlike status. For some, this means that if the index is up 20%, you should be higher, and incidentally 1% higher is often terrific, because most managers struggling with index-related performance stay close to S&P weightings and characteristics anyway. If the index is down 20% and you are down "only" 15%, it's a "home run." In other words, losing money can be rationalized if the bogey is an index. This is another flaw of indexation unless you firmly believe that indices have a permanent upward bias or, more importantly, that they go up when you are invested.

Index names change and new ones appear from time to time to reflect new markets or their constituent parts. As global markets expand further, we will see even more indices.

Remember, however, that the securities that comprise the indices have to change over time to reflect mergers, acquisitions, insolvencies, and other events. In essence, indices themselves are not quite the rigid, unchanging standards of investment competence that the name suggests because they too try to "manage themselves" in order to look right in a changing environment.

In their defense, however, indices are often the representative beacons of their respective markets. In other words, we may argue over the value of active versus passive management of assets but rarely ever debate the relevance of a specific index to the underlying market that it purports to represent. If we accept that as true for traditional markets, what can be said about an index for hedge funds?

NORMAL PORTFOLIOS

Before answering, let's continue with traditional areas for just a bit longer by touching briefly on the *normal portfolio,* which is essentially a tailor-made benchmark for an individual manager. By identifying a working universe of stocks on the basis of a manager's screening criteria—let's say, 200—we now have an "index." The manager's actual portfolios may contain 30 to 50 stocks at any time, the performance of which reflects his active management. Comparing these results with that of his normal portfolio determines whether the manager has added value. Normal portfolios are most appropriate for somewhat eclectic managers or those who otherwise should not be judged against an index such as the S&P 500—which as we have shown, is an index dominated by large capitalization U.S. stocks. For example, a manager who exclusively uses stocks of companies that are in the bottom quintile of the S&P 500 (that is, small capitalization stocks) would have 100% of his portfolio in issues that were only 2% of the index. Clearly this is a case for a normal portfolio or the use of another index.

Indices also can be tailored to and, to some degree, derived from managed assets. Indeed, when we want to compare a money manager with other managers, we assemble a group utilizing similar styles or approaches and rank them. Though we typically include an actual index in the rankings, the database constructed of manager performance itself becomes an index of sorts by indicating whether your manager did a good or bad job versus his peers.

Some people even construct a normal portfolio for their total fund by combining asset classes. Suppose you have a total fund with five managers who themselves manage five different asset classes for you. Let's say one invests in large capitalization U.S. equity, another in small capitalization U.S. equity, a third in non-U.S. equity in major industrialized countries, a fourth in emerging markets, and the last in U.S. bonds. Clearly you would need five separate indices or normal portfolios to judge each manager, and five separate databases of peer group managers for each asset class. But what about the total fund? Should you use each of the five indices in tailored or arbitrary weightings to generate an index, or tailored or arbitrary weightings of the median manager in each peer group universe? An easy but not necessarily logical solution is to assemble a "universe of total funds" and simply rank your fund among them regardless of differential asset class weightings of the various total funds in the universe.

A more sophisticated player might combine the five relevant indices or normal portfolios into a superindex or supernormal that truly reflects "the ponds they are fishing in." Still, how do you weight the indices? Equally, by dollars allocated, or by size of the markets they represent? Many different answers are possible and even right, but the message is the same. Indices are useful but imperfect and often don't stretch to reflect the competence and representation that they seek to isolate. More often than not they don't reach, and we must build a bridge to close the gap between the general and the specific. Such is the case with hedge funds, which for the most part defy indexation or normal portfolios. Even worse, when peer group databases are assembled, the underlying funds' wide diversity of both content and strategy inhibits meaningful comparisons. How then do you get a quick, handy measure of what's happening in the field?

THE EACM 100^{SM} INDEX

Investors all too often simply reach for a generally accepted index such as the S&P 500 for a quick reference on hedge funds. Most of the time such comparisons are meaningless and, at worst, misleading. If hedge funds are supposed to be equity-type investments, what alternatives do investors have other than a U.S. equity index? Normal portfolios certainly are not the readily available solution.

The world of hedge funds does not have a true index, and our guess is that the diversity in markets and strategies generally found therein will hinder any rapid development of widely accepted indices. The potential impacts of shorting, leverage, hedging, and other techniques characteristic of hedge fund investing further complicate the issue. The task loses its enormity only in hindsight, when in the progression of performance evaluation techniques in the 1960s, we looked more to competitive performance data among managers as a prelude to the development of indices as a genuinely integral part of what made a manager's results competitive. Competitiveness, after all, seems to be the goal of all performance comparisons.

The diversity of asset classes in use by institutions and high net worth investors is increasing, as are the subset strategy groupings within asset classes. At the same time, rules for mutual funds have been expanded which will permit new entrants to hedge fund management. Additional potential for closed-end funds here and elsewhere also exists, bringing hedge fund returns more and more into the public domain. Accordingly, the numbers of all sorts of specifically relevant indices and manager database comparisons will grow.

In the meantime, hedge funds have no generally accepted index and therefore lack the ready reference that modern investors use to identify a market. Though a hedge fund index seems unlikely and problematical in the near future, a need nonetheless exists for a series of indicators that describe what is happening in that world of diverse strategies. Investors would benefit from a quick reference or window, if you will, that effectively acts as a hybrid between an index and a performance database.

Perfection cannot be the goal of a hedge fund index or the index will fail from the start. The hedge fund manager's palette is too diverse. Nevertheless, a generally accepted barometer is needed, and the following will outline the methodology of one such approach, the EACM 100.

The EACM index was designed to represent a "sampling" of the alternative strategies universe with a group of 100 professional investment management organizations. Designed as an investible index, the weightings of the various strategies reflect judgments based on the availability of investment talent and the risk preferences of institutionally oriented investors. The manager selection is biased toward identifying good professionally managed operations that are generally representative of the relevant investment style or strategy. A crucial element of the selection process was to make no attempt to identify "stars" or "gems." The EACM index thus seeks to represent a natural "base case" portfolio of alternative managers with substantial room for added value through either strategy allocation or manager selection, or both.

EACM 100 Construct

As indicated above, the construct of the EACM 100 starts with a judgment call that determines the percentage in each hedge fund strategy and substrategy. The percentage is based on an analysis of the assets at work in the field, as well as the number of operating practitioners in each strategy.

The following are general guidelines for manager selection in the index:

- ◆ Managers must have at least a one-year performance record and a minimum of $20 million in assets under management. (At this writing, index managers have a median assets under management and track record of $200 million and 7.5 years, respectively.)
- ◆ Managers must be open for investment and provide timely data relevant to performance of their funds.
- ◆ Managers must meet some critical level of credibility and substance, but need not be of "gem" quality.

Conversely, the general criteria for removing a manager from the index (on a forward basis) include a change in basic strategy, a lack of cooperation or timeliness in providing data, a drop in assets below the minimum required, closure of the shop to new assets, or closure of the shop or partnership to all business activity in general.

As with any index, we should be sure to question the issue of survivor bias. The EACM 100 Index was compiled in 1995 with the benefit of hindsight, and with the requirement that the constituent managers be investible, resulting in the inclusion of appropriate managers existing at that time (and the exclusion of vehicles which had previously been terminated). From that point forward, however, when a manager is closed or terminated for market or strategic reasons, the history of that manager remains in the index forever. Likewise, when new managers are introduced to the index, the adoption date marks the inception of the series: The index is not restated to reflect the historical performance of the new managers. Given these parameters, beginning with its public debut in January 1996, the EACM 100 is cited as an investible index.

Of the 100 managers comprising the index, 50% represent "specialty strategies"—that is, Relative Value, Event Driven, and Short Selling. The other 50% represent the broad-based strategies—namely, Equity Hedge and Global Asset Allocators.

Quantitative Characteristics

To put the EACM 100 in perspective, let's focus first on Exhibit 7–1, which shows the risk/return characteristics of the EACM, the constituent hedge fund strategies, and selected other asset classes over the period 1990–1996. A purist might legitimately argue that hedge fund strategies are far from homogeneous, *within* as well as *among* strategies, thus diminishing the value of an index. Remember, "generally representative" was the goal, not perfection.

Exhibit 7–2 shows the correlation of returns over the same period as that examined in Exhibit 7–1. Remember, 1.00 is a perfect positive correlation and –1.00 a perfect negative correlation. As an admittedly general conclusion, very little

E X H I B I T   7–1

Historical Risk/Return: 1990–1996

Sources: EACM 100^{SM} Index and Sub-groups, Standard & Poor's, Morgan Stanley Capital International, Lehman Brothers, Merrill Lynch.

relates to anything else. Hedge funds appear to be very different creatures from the S&P 500, both individually and as represented by the EACM.

Though somewhat overwhelming in terms of the numbers, Exhibit 7–3 effectively restates Exhibit 7–1 while taking you a little further into the innards of risk and return. The lower standard deviation of the EACM 100 relative to the S&P 500 is captured in both the lower upside (maximum three months) and downside (minimum three months) three-month periods. Shorting suffers over the full period, but notice the positive volatility on the upside (downside for the stock market). Relative value, further, dances to its own drum with a far lower standard deviation than most of the other strategies.

Lest we forget that "one standard deviation does not risk make," particularly when using manager averages for

EXHIBIT   7-2

Correlation of Monthly Returns: 1990–1996

	EACM 100[SM]	Relative Value	Event Driven	Equity Hedge	Global AA	Short Selling	S&P 500
EACM 100[SM]	1.00						
Relative Value	0.48	1.00					
Event Driven	0.35	0.26	1.00				
Equity Hedge	0.52	0.26	0.59	1.00			
Global AA	0.77	0.13	−0.12	−0.03	1.00		
Short Selling	−0.06	−0.07	−0.56	−0.72	0.25	1.00	
S&P 500	0.26	−0.02	0.47	0.68	0.00	−0.73	1.00

Sources: EACM 100[SM] Index and Sub-groups, Standard & Poor's.

EXHIBIT   7-3

Performance Characteristics: 1990–1996

	EACM 100[SM]	Relative Value	Event Driven	Equity Hedge	Global AA	Short Selling	S&P 500
Return	17.0	12.7	14.7	20.1	24.6	−3.6	14.4
Std. Deviation	3.4	2.3	5.0	6.6	12.0	22.2	11.6
Max. Month	4.7	2.8	5.1	5.4	16.4	17.5	11.4
Max. 3 Months	7.6	6.2	11.6	13.4	20.5	34.1	16.7
Min. Month	−0.9	−1.1	−4.8	−3.9	−5.5	−13.0	−9.1
Min. 3 Months	−1.1	−1.7	−7.5	−4.3	−4.3	−25.6	−13.8
Annual Periods							
1990	18.4	10.8	−0.5	11.3	50.1	51.2	−3.1
1991	25.0	15.8	23.1	37.3	36.9	−25.0	30.4
1992	15.6	15.2	14.9	16.1	20.7	−5.9	7.6
1993	23.1	15.7	26.8	31.3	28.2	−9.2	10.1
1994	3.6	1.3	7.1	3.1	0.8	17.7	1.3
1995	17.0	16.2	17.8	22.4	20.9	−23.9	37.6
1996	17.3	14.6	15.7	22.6	20.4	−10.6	22.9

Sources: EACM 100[SM] Index and Sub-groups, Standard & Poor's.

data points, Exhibit 7–4 focuses on the issue of one standard deviation as a measure of risk. Importantly, hedge funds are a volatile and risky asset class, but the S&P 500, if you believe that the index has relevance to hedge funds, is also no "walk in the park." Almost any type of investing involves risk of loss, or at least some negative surprises at times. From Exhibit 7–4, note particularly the periods when each strategy, as well as the S&P 500, moves outside the bounds of one standard deviation over the seven-year period.

In any asset class, an index is designed to indicate or signal something relative to the performance of its underlying markets. As we have discussed, an index can take a variety of forms—a normal portfolio, a standard index, or a combination of indices. Any of these configurations is essentially a diversified portfolio designed to be a barometer for relative performance.

Peer group comparisons unfortunately invite a sense of averaging manager results rather than referencing a true index, which in fact can be significantly above or below the "average." You might compare individual managers against a strategy universe that is much broader than the EACM indexes. In contrast, the EACM 100, with others and those to follow, offers on a combined basis some sense of what hedge funds in general are doing. It is akin to turning on a light in a dark room and struggling to get more lights to follow. The component strategy results within the EACM 100 may or may not represent "the average manager," but if objectively chosen to be generally representative of the strategy itself, the EACM 100 is a reasonable barometer of what is happening and, for now, a useful albeit imperfect "index."

At the end of the day, the adequacy of hedge fund performance needs to be examined on various levels against different premises:

EXHIBIT   7–4 a, b, c

Trailing Annual Returns

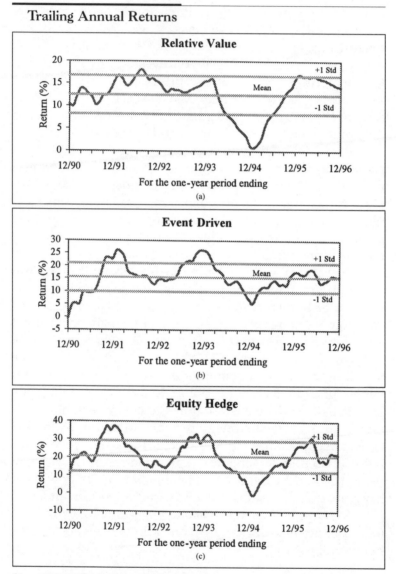

(a)

(b)

(c)

Sources: EACM 100^{SM} Index Sub-groups, Standard & Poor's.

E X H I B I T   7–4 d, e, f

Trailing Annual Returns

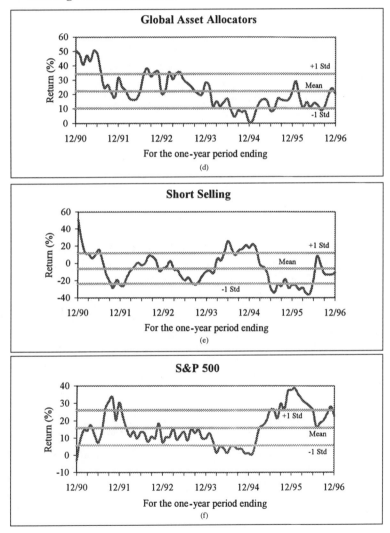

Sources: EACM 100^{SM} Index Sub-groups, Standard & Poor's.

- ◆ Versus traditional assets: "Am I in the right asset class?"
- ◆ Versus other alternative or nontraditional assets: "Am I in the right strategy?"
- ◆ Versus other hedge fund managers of the same strategy: "Am I with the best manager?"
- ◆ Versus risk-adjusted returns: "Am I with the best manager in the right asset class on a risk-adjusted basis?"

Whatever the consideration, the availability of a reference point is an integral part of the comparison, pointing to the need for a genuine group of indices in the hedge fund arena, and soon. The creation of such indices will be no easy task, and as suggested many times above, it may be long in coming. Though the problem may seem simple in retrospect, we recall the early 1960s and the many debates over the applicability of the S&P 500 as an institutionally oriented U.S. equity index. Fierce debate raged over this index even through the 1970s. The experience of the past perhaps sheds some light on the role of a new index, which is to "stick its neck out," despite its imperfections, and help focus the professional community on an important need. The indices in use today may be less representative than many would like, but they nonetheless exist.

SUMMARY AND COMMENTS

1. Index-type comparisons are not available for hedge fund performance, and may never exist in "perfect" form, but their absence makes evaluation difficult.

2. Normal portfolios provide a tighter fit for comparison purposes, but the eclectic nature of hedge funds, as well

as their tendency toward secrecy of portfolio strategy and content, probably precludes their creation in the short run.

3. Performance indices such as the EACM 100 are an interim solution and as close as we can get to an index at this time. Reporting strategies on an individual basis is an important first step in the evolution toward an acceptable and effective index.

4. Risk is too often a missing dimension to hedge fund comparisons, and standard deviation measurements seem woefully lacking in the world of leverage and shorting.

CHAPTER 8

The Future
of Institutional
Investment in
Hedge Funds

Let's start by defining institutions as U.S. pension and endowment funds and their approximately $6 trillion in total assets under management. Let's further assume the possibility that institutions invest 2% to 3% of total fund assets in hedge funds over the next 10 years, or $100–200 billion. (We estimate that hedge fund assets under management at present are about $300–400 billion.)

RAMIFICATIONS OF INCREASING
INSTITUTIONAL ASSETS
IN HEDGE FUNDS

If our estimate is close to accurate, the increase in institutional assets will have a dramatic impact not only on the hedge fund business but on the conduct of institutional fund management as well. Consider the following.

1. The number of hedge funds will increase, and the only gauge we have from the past is the tremendous growth in registered investment advisers from roughly 3000 to 21,000 over the last 25 to 30 years as positive asset flows into the markets persisted. Our estimates are of some 4000 to 5000 hedge funds now, with brokerage houses and traditional money management firms providing a pool of professionals to fuel further growth. The geographic concentration of hedge funds in the U.S. northeast will lessen, and non-U.S. practitioners will increase.

2. Though a few hedge fund "complexes" are as big as $12–15 billion now, the vast majority are well under $300 million. Clearly, many hedge fund managers will grow in asset and organizational size. A key question is whether results will suffer, and that is too early to assess. Expansive growth of any asset management organization is a worry, but no one to our knowledge has yet been able to definitively relate size to performance, particularly in a venue of expanding global markets.

Don't underestimate the impact of strategic partnership relationships ("one-stop shopping") that some large institutional funds are featuring. In the 1950s and early 1960s, single balanced investment managers managed institutional assets with an orientation that was almost exclusively U.S. securities. The acceptance of indices, the growth in investment consultants, and the failure of domestic balanced managers to demonstrate asset allocation skills spurred fund sponsors to hire managers for specialized asset class assignments. A reversal is currently taking place with the challenge to fiduciary committees and consultants to deal knowledgeably and opportunistically with asset allocation issues and, as a compounding factor, the growth in global markets. Strategic management relationships with global balanced managers are once again being initiated.

One could argue that among hedge funds, Global Asset Allocators are in the same business as global balanced managers, searching for returns across markets unlimited by investment techniques or instruments. Curiously, we believe that over time an institutionally driven merger of shorting and leverage into long equity-type investing will occur, in effect blending hedge fund approaches with traditional investment. Though specialists and differentiation of managers by asset class always will exist, the prototypical manager of the distant future is the one for which the distinction beween *traditional* and *nontraditional* will not be important. Hedge funds thus bring the philosophic reacceptance of global balanced management a step closer.

3. Hedge funds will gradually assume many of the characteristics of traditional money management. Future hedge fund investors will likely experience more separate accounts, greater transparency of portfolios, more and better risk monitoring systems, and lower fees.

4. Regulation of hedge funds will increase, with more scrutiny by regulatory bodies, political entities, and other interested third parties.

5. Stockbrokers will be forced to expand and increase the sophistication of their services to hedge funds. Demands on capital and expertise necessary to participate in new global arenas may result in only a handful of stockbrokers, few more than now exist, who specialize in the main-line servicing of hedge funds.

6. Fund sponsors will undergo a radical change in investment perspective, particularly in how they judge their traditional equity and fixed income components. Why is market timing impossible? Why not hedge? Is UBTI really such a big bogeyman? Are performance fees all that bad?

INCENTIVES TO INCREASE INSTITUTIONAL ASSETS IN HEDGE FUNDS

Any number of events may trigger increasing institutional participation in hedge funds, but here are some possibilities.

1. The movement toward employee choice plans will continue and place greater pressure on defined benefit plans and manager performance as new cash flows decline and early retirements proliferate. Further, there is pressure on foundation and endowment funds to supplement operating budgets with investment gains, and that will not diminish.

2. At this writing, U.S. equity markets are full by many measures, an omen that a retrenchment may lie ahead. No guarantees exist, but if hedge funds outperform traditional equity management on the downside, investors will direct a lot of attention to that area.

3. Even if no downturn occurs, fund sponsors have a natural propensity to look over the fence for new, perhaps better, opportunities. Equally so, fund sponsors get tired of traditional money managers taking them for granted, particularly if those managers are underperforming the S&P 500.

4. Changes in hedge fund eligibility limitations, such as seen in recent legislative actions, will make hedge funds more accessible to prospective investors.

5. Investment consultants who advise the vast bulk of leading foundations and endowments, as well as the majority of Fortune 1000 company pension funds, may exert pressure on their clients to expand alternative investments.

6. Traditional money managers with successful records and institutional clientele are already leaving established firms to start their own hedge funds. In response to this logical progression, traditional management companies are considering in-house hedge funds to keep key people.

Hedge fund general partners who are attempting to attract institutional clients have often lamented the absence of institutional interest, all based on the general partner's reality of a good performance year. The institutional fund sponsor has a much more complex set of parameters with which to deal before gaining an interest. Hedge fund managers, often the ultimate rugged individualists, must learn to adapt, picture, and posture themselves in a manner more acceptable to this new buyer in order to accelerate the integration.

THE INSTITUTIONAL VIEW OF THE HEDGE FUND

It is important to understand the institutional view of the hedge fund, and that begins with an examination of style. There are many ways to look at traditional equity style analysis, but they are all based on the three major contributors to risk and return: market, sector, and company. A simple matrix is shown in Exhibit 8–1.

From the left-hand Market axis, Active refers to heavy market timers, Moderate to medium market timers, and Minimal just as the name implies. Sector deals with economic, industry, or other group segmentations of the market, and the same timing logic applies—that is, Active refers to a heavy rotational approach to sector weightings, while Moderate and Minimal are to be taken in the obvious context. Inside each of the nine boxes (Active-Active, Minimal-Moderate, etc.), there are four further segmentations representing Growth, Value, Emerging Growth, and Eclectic. As such, a buy-and-hold, small capitalization, high-technology manager would be in the lower-right-hand box under Emerging Growth, and a value investor who is moderately oriented to both market timing and sector rotation would be in the center box under

E X H I B I T   8–1

Traditional Equity Styles

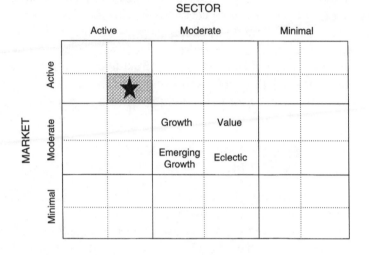

Value. The vast bulk of traditional domestic equity managers fall in the middle (Moderate-Moderate) of the matrix, leaning toward the lower Minimal-Moderate level. Most are growth or value, and very few eclectic.

Hedge funds certainly differ one to the other, but Equity Hedge funds and Global Asset Allocators, for example, would fall in the Active-Active box under Eclectic. Few, if any, traditional managers appear in that box. Hedge funds are clearly a different approach and, therefore, a potentially effective diversifier. Further, managers in the upper-left-hand box might be expected not only to be opportunistic but probably to time markets and their rotations imperfectly and, in so doing, underperform in sustained, upward moves and outperform in those that are negative.

The very heavy orientation of institutional portfolios to the S&P 500 has a few implications worth considering. The first is that in a sustained bear market, most traditional managers (as well as many hedge funds) will be down. Equally confusing is the probability that active management of traditional equity assets will outperform the S&P 500, maybe significantly so. There will even be traditional market timers who finally get it right, and perennial bears who have their moment in the sun. The latter will be the messiahs, drawing large crowds as in 1973–1974, who will have great difficulty getting back in and likely will miss much of the recovery. Amidst all this noise, will institutional investors head for the Mecca of hedge funds? The answer is some, not all, but their assets could be meaningful. People tend to forget how large some institutional funds are and how powerful their movements can be.

INDICATIONS OF INSTITUTIONAL INVESTMENT IN HEDGE FUNDS

The beginnings of the institutional move into hedge funds has begun with endowments and foundations moving more aggressively than corporate and public investors. High-profile beauty shows will follow, where leading-edge institutional investors screen for the "best managers." At this writing, we have never had so many inquiries about hedge fund managers and what they do. Equally telling is the growth in the number of new "fund of funds" structures using hedge funds, with some sponsored by foreign and domestic banks.

What do you do if you are an institutional investor? Prepare to adjust your thinking about how assets are managed and clients are handled. What do you do if you are a hedge fund manager? Something very close to the same

answer. This will be a gentle collision but collision nevertheless, and much will change in the process.

In Exhibit 8–2, Greenwich Associates, a business strategy research and consulting firm that also collects and pub-
lishes data on investment-related trends, describes the state
of the field in 1996:

Exhibit 8–2 differentiates among corporate, public, and
endowment funds and their use of buyout funds, hedge
funds, and venture capital. The exhibit shows the following
investment levels in hedge funds for the three types of funds:

Corporate	Public	Endowments
3%	2%	29%

It is not hard to see where the action in hedge funds has
been (and is), but our bet is that future corporate and public
fund interest will rival that of endowments. The list will also
broaden to reflect more names and less domination by the
major endowment players of today.

E X H I B I T   8–2

Demand for Alternative Investments

| | Buyout Funds | | | Hedge Funds | | | Venture Capital | | |
	Now Use	Would Consider	Total Demand	Now Use	Would Consider	Total Demand	Now Use	Would Consider	Total Demand
Corporate funds	6%	2%	8%	3%	4%	7%	14%	2%	16%
Public funds	5%	2%	7%	2%	2%	4%	17%	4%	21%
Endowments	26%	8%	33%	29%	12%	40%	41%	9%	50%
TOTAL FUNDS	9%	3%	12%	7%	5%	11%	19%	3%	22%

Source: Greenwich Associates

LIKELY INTEREST BY
SPECIFIC STRATEGIES

At this point, let us once again disaggregate hedge funds into their component parts in order to differentiate them as likely portals through which institutions might enter.

Relative Value

Relative Value is a natural entry point, but not in all its subcategories:

1. *Long/short equity* is something of a natural, because many strategies are driven by valuation systems that institutions can understand. Shorting and leverage (if used) would be a hurdle but countered on the positive side by the potential for low relative volatility of returns born of hedged positions.

2. *Convertible arbitrage* is not quite the same, because convertibles tend to be lower credits, and the shorting of stocks is a "soft" attempt to hedge. It also tends to add a market timing flavor to setting the hedge ratio. Leverage and the possibility of the hedge being very wrong may dampen investor enthusiasm for this strategy.

3. *Bond hedging* requires substantial leverage as a core element and that itself may be enough to discourage potential investors.

Short Selling

As a stand-alone strategy rather than part of a hedged transaction, as with long/short equity or convertible arbitrage, Short Selling may be a nonstarter because of an ingrained corporate bias against the activity itself. Shorting also may be very difficult to do in huge institutional size, and the practitioners themselves are few, with some not having endeared themselves to corporate issuers over the years.

Event Driven

Event Driven strategies create public relations issues for corporate investors, but not as much for endowments and foundations. Many corporate pension funds have a natural reluctance to invest in hostile takeovers or to engage in "vulture investing."

Equity Hedge and GAA

Equity Hedge funds and Global Asset Allocators are the most likely magnets for institutional assets. As the stereotypical "hedge funds" with the longer-tenured and more well-known practitioners, they can put relatively large assets to work, and they have a palette large enough to conform to special institutional requests.

Regardless of the strategy, how does a hedge fund communicate its message when bound so tightly by regulatory limitations? Many hedge funds have designated marketing people (perhaps not identified quite as such), others use speeches, articles, and other measures to get their message across. Unlike the usual traditional asset management sales process, hedge funds cannot depend on unsolicited cold calls to attract institutional investment. In many ways, hedge fund marketing will have to fight the natural urge to be "independent and tough" and help the potential buyer to the table.

HEDGE FUNDS VS. OTHER FORMS OF ALTERNATIVE INVESTMENTS

Having now been introduced to the world of hedge fund investing and perhaps ready to consider a step beyond traditional main-line investing, you might legitimately question the advantages or differences between hedge funds and other types of alternative investments. Clearly, the Greenwich Associates data (Exhibit 8–2) indicate that institutions, particularly endowment funds, use venture capital far more than any other alternative asset class. Why then hedge funds? Why not venture capital?

Venture capital and private equity investments, the largest representatives in the alternative classification, are really quite small as a percentage of institutional total fund portfolios. Together with hedge funds and other types of alternative investments, it is doubtful that venture capital and private equity ever will cross the bridge to widespread institutional acceptance and use. Still, investors have legitimized venture capitalists by virtue of their gutsy, all-American image of investing in small companies or revitalized struggling ones, and hitting some home runs in the process.

There are good reasons that some institutional funds have had a preference for venture capital and private equity investments. These strategies are almost always long a security (usually equity or an equivalent) and, except for some possible hedging, never short. For the most part, leverage is embedded inside the acquired company, so UBTI is not a concern. And, relative to public equity markets, venture capital and private equity offer the potential for above-average returns and diversification.

There are also negative features associated with these strategies. Venture capital and private equity investments almost always involve lockups of 5 to 15 years, and annual management fees of perhaps 2% with a 20% carry for the general partner. Although the portfolios are transparent to the investor, these companies are not the kinds of investments that enable a limited partner to learn all there is to know from an industry "tear sheet." Communication from the general partner may also depart greatly from the ideal. One of the biggest unknowns is how good the general partner is, and whether he can buy well and catch a favorable exit door in a cycle that he does not control.

Keep in mind that the dispersion of returns is high among partnerships with the same vintage years (the latter denoting investing partnership offerings that commence in a specific year), making a strong case for manager selection. Equally important, and in terms of returns themselves, is the vintage year in which you invest. Some venture capitalists/private equity investors shoot the lights out because exit environments are so good. Given that an institutional fund does not invest in venture or deal partnerships each year, dollar cost averaging rarely smoothes out results. Rather, on the basis of manager reputation and with limited information at hand, institutions periodically leap in for perhaps ±10 years and hope for the best.

Averaging venture and private equity returns over many vintage years and exit periods surprisingly indicates, by our estimates, average annual returns in the mid-teens, net of all fees. Though some expect returns closer to 25%, the mid-teens seem a fair representation of the median or average over extended periods. Curiously, the mid-teens seems to be a reasonable expectation for results of other alternative and nontraditional strategies as well. Even though the S&P 500 returns over the last 15 years or so have been in the same range, 15% is acceptable relative to historical public equity returns in the United States.

If returns from public and private market investing are expected to be the same, why accept above-average fees and lockups when you can just buy an index? The reasons are obvious and myriad, beginning with "you never know in advance," and importantly, returns can be much larger if your timing and/or company selection is right. Alternative investing thus has a clear place in an institutional total fund for many reasons, and hedge funds are an essential part of the picture. The fact that only a very few hedge funds require more than a one-year lockup, and many offer monthly or quarterly liquidity, is a key focal point.

Alternative investing typically needs a long horizon to play out in the most opportunistic fashion. For example, timber needs to be bought for cash, grown, and sold when the housing cycle is strong, and venture cap needs a strong IPO market to survive. We would argue that lockups prevent investors from pulling out at the wrong time, but they also place assets at risk for a long time without the fund sponsor having any control. That is a great leap of faith for most, so why not take all your targeted venture capital and private equity dollars and put them in hedge funds? The answer is that they play different roles and often march to different drums. Let's summarize some of the major similarities and differences:

- ◆ The charter of venture and private equity is very defined as to sector, industry, or approach and possibly to all of those combined; hedge funds, especially Global Asset Allocators and Equity Hedge funds, are more eclectic. Out of 10 investments with venture and private equity you generally can expect 2 home runs and 2 total busts, with the remaining 6 a little above or below average. Further, if previous partnerships are still in operation, they may contain individual holdings that the general partner has valued. Hedge funds would have great difficulty staying in business with a "2 out of 10 hit ratio" and too many issues valued by the partner.

◆ Although private equity often ends in public equity holdings, its charter is mostly private. Hedge funds, on the other hand, can hold thinly traded and, in some cases, even private issues, but the latter are generally at a minimum.

◆ For the most part, leverage increases risk. Even allowing that private equity has its leverage embedded in the operating companies, risk is a significant item for institutions to recognize when utilizing hedge funds.

◆ High fees breed a low tolerance for poor performance with hedge funds; the same would be true for venture and private equity without the long-term lockup.

◆ Regulatory oversight and governance are an added comfort to investors. Unless changes in this area occur, the fact that hedge funds and private equity structures lack such protection may relegate them permanently to an alternative status.

◆ Venture capital and private equity are long-biased strategies with definite elements of market risk and sensitivity to economic cycles. Hedge funds can use short selling and other techniques to dampen this connection to the standard market environment.

In our view, venture capital, private equity, and hedge funds deserve a position in an institutional investment program for some very different reasons. Returns and diversification surely are the expectation for all of them, but totally different educational processes are of immense value as well. It is important that a fund sponsor realize that alternative investments demand a lot of time relative to the small percentage of a total fund they represent. For the sake of argument, let's take a $1 billion fund that can have a maximum of 10% of the fund, or $100 million, allocated to alternative asset classes. Suppose that 2% to 3%, or $20–30 million, is allocated to multiple hedge funds using a diversified strategy, and the remainder to other alternative classes such as venture, private equity, timber, and oil and gas. A cynic could take the view that even $30 million making 15% is only adding $4.5 million, or less than 0.5%, to the total fund in a given year. Why try? And, by the way, this "small investment" will take a disproportionate amount of time to evaluate, select, and monitor. The math is correct, but there are some other items to consider:

- ◆ The "alternative" component must be taken as a whole. For illustrative purposes, using the same math, 15% on $100 million is $15 million, or 1.5% add-on to the total fund—not at all insignificant.
- ◆ The lower correlation of hedge funds (and other alternative investments) with the S&P 500 may dampen the volatility of the total fund and soften on the downside.
- ◆ Learning about and understanding the investment environment as a whole is part of the process as well. You can't know too much, and hedge fund and venture/private equity managers have much to teach.
- ◆ There is nothing magical about a 10% allocation to alternative investments, and several major institutions have been operating at or above the 25% level for many years.

Alternative investing has its successes and failures. This book seeks not to give legal advice or, for that matter, investment advice, because each individual situation will be different. In general, we are as much in favor of hedge funds for institutional and high net worth investment programs as we are venture and private equity. Still, alternative investing is not mainstream and, as such, holds the potential for inefficiencies that can lead to good rates of return. Accordingly, responsible fiduciary considerations always apply, but under the right circumstances, hedge funds and venture/private equity can fit and do so nicely.

SUMMARY AND COMMENTS

1. There are signs of significant institutional interest in hedge funds but no dramatic flow of funds yet. When and if such growth begins, it will move at a measured, possibly somewhat intermittent, pace.

2. Profound structural and functional changes in the hedge fund industry will occur in the event institutional interest becomes a reality. Some changes will be good and others bad. Both the hedge funds and the fund sponsors will need to help one another across bridges not yet built. Regulators will be drawn in as well.

3. History imparts a lot of wisdom if you follow the course of institutional funds and the profound changes that have occurred over the past decades. When skeptics think nothing has changed, note that insurance companies "owned" the pension investment management business in the 1950s and that equity investment was rare. Banks dominated the "new" equity management in the 1960s, independent firms started in the late 1960s, and active bond management commenced around 1970. As of that date, real estate, international, and emerging markets were among the non-starters.

The acceptance and use of new asset classes are in large measure a creative response to differing demands of fund sponsor needs. A greater move toward hedge funds would not be a large step in the perspective of history.

Summary and Conclusions

This book was written as a primer and not as a definitive text, because all too often the definitive text inflicts massive amounts of data without imparting real learning. In fact, we endeavored to sketch out the skeleton with just enough flesh to give it form, with the missing pieces a beating heart and flowing blood to make the body live. To take that next step involves a trade-by-trade analysis of hedge funds, which, as with any investment portfolio discussion, takes time and space. For us that may be the next book, but for the reader, no sense of shortfall should exist. Rather, there is unfinished work to do, perhaps best accomplished by paying due diligence to actual investment vehicles.

As said in so many ways, hedge fund investing is for the qualified and sophisticated investor who can tolerate the total loss of invested assets and, as this book has emphasized, is best implemented in a diversified manner with a small percentage of total fund assets. Either way, multiple partnerships and general partners is the underlying principle.

Hedge funds defy the homogeneity that conventional wisdom has attributed to them, reflecting instead distinct strategy and cultural differences. They are in large measure eclectic in nature and by charter, which means that you must understand that they have authority to pursue opportunity wherever and whenever perceived using whatever instruments are at their command. Hedge fund managers are people with all the usual distractions of life and the capability of both good and bad days. Yet all the while they charge relatively high fees, implying excellence that may not be present at any given time. Institutional and other sophisticated investors too often mistake their small investment (relative to total fund) to be a license to homogenize the asset class. To do so runs the risk of disappointment even when returns are good, because expectations were different.

Hedge fund managers can be tough to like, but it is difficult not to admire the great confidence and faith that they have in themselves, demonstrated by the willingness to risk their futures on their skills. The desire to draw a salary and benefit package simply does not exist. Hedge fund managers can also be hard-nosed businesspeople, with the nose becoming harder as good performance drives growth in assets under management. However, let's not overromanticize the fact that "we are partners," because in the final analysis they sell a service and you buy it (or not). Putting it another way, you are a spectator and they are the players, using *your* ball, so don't mistake the term *partner* for something other than *investor*.

Performance fees are a standard operating characteristic of hedge funds. As for investment characteristics, hedge funds are long and short and some even try to be hedged. They use securities, futures, forwards, options, structured instruments, physicals, private securities, and whatever else is on the table, levered or not, in any country of the world. That can be fine, even laudable, if you know them and trust their skills. Be careful, however, because some overconfident or overaggressive managers may venture forth without the skills or staff.

General partners are motivated by making money for themselves and for you, in that order. Risk is high and stress is great; they earn their pay in part because they extend themselves to extremes to make money. As a rule, general partners are in the prime of life with good experience and schooling and, filled with the zest born of that profile, assume the role of enthusiastic gladiators wrestling with the markets, themselves, and you. "Cruise control" is not part of their being.

Investors endure hedge funds because they seek high returns and diversification from more traditional asset classes. Compiling returns net of fees is often no mean task, but it is an essential calculation for true comparisons and, of course, net returns to the investor. Strange as it may seem, if the S&P 500, or whatever representative traditional index you choose, can render 15%± per year net, then hedge funds and other forms of nontraditional investments will have a problem competing. Excluding the Relative Value strategy, which seeks returns modestly above those of three-month Treasury bills, hedge funds must give you 15% per year on average or the asset class is a nonstarter. Regarding diversification of returns, it is difficult to generalize about the correlation of hedge funds with traditional markets. The relationship between returns of the two asset classes requires constant attention, particularly in periods of extreme market movements, up or down. Low correlation and possible diversification is a factor here but not the primary consideration when considering hedge funds.

If you are a taxable investor, be very attentive to after-tax returns. Taxes have an enormous negative impact on compounding returns. If you are a tax-exempt investor, be attentive to taxes as well because the predominance of hedge fund investors, and indeed the general partners themselves, are taxable investors. As such, tax-effective management may not ultimately be in the interest of maximum pretax total return.

We have identified five types of hedge fund strategies throughout the book, and it is important to understand the differences among them. We have emphasized that, at times, the somewhat eclectic approach used by different general partners causes wide dispersion of results, even among managers categorized in the same strategy grouping. In essence, you need to understand the strategy you want, select carefully the manager to deliver the strategy, and stay close to him thereafter.

If you knew a partnership would make you a lot of money in a given year but also had a 30% standard deviation, you might well invest in it. On the other hand, if you knew one that would lose you money but had a low standard deviation, you probably would not. Risk is really measured in the potential for losing money, not volatility of returns. Not knowing results in advance makes us look to, and too often rely on, such measures as past volatility.

Diversification across multiple managers can help to reduce risk. Other items that contribute to the risk of losing money are hedging (or the lack thereof), leverage, liquidity, general partner health and well-being, among others. All add to that feeling in your stomach which, in the final analysis, is the ultimate decision maker in assessing risk. In sum, you really need to trust the general partner and invest a limited amount of your assets, preferably with multiple managers.

Investing in hedge funds is an unnerving exercise in itself. Partnership agreements are often grossly one-sided and, in our view, can reflect the real modus operandi of the general partner. If you have to read a page twice to understand the terms, be careful. Yet too many people don't read the documents (even certifying that they have) and more don't take the time to understand them. Use your legal and accounting professionals. Provisions are clear if you get some legal help, and often can be understood with your own intensive concentration. Never assume that terms are nonnegotiable, particularly if you are a sizable investor.

Fees are everyone's hot button. If you invest in a $300 million hedge fund, for example, and it is up 20% in a given year, the general partner's gross compensation is $15 million (based on 1% management fee plus 20% incentive). After paying his staff and miscellaneous expenses, he takes home $12 million, which is two or three times what your corporation's president makes. The general partner does not give money back if he has negative returns. In effect, he uses your money to invest to make himself rich, and the vehicle that empowers him is the partnership agreement. Therefore, review it very carefully with your professional advisors and negotiate where you can.

Evaluating hedge fund managers is one of the joys and challenges of life. In doing so you must visit, you must analyze, and you must rank by conviction, not by performance or cocktail party touts. You will not be disappointed, because these managers are never boring, and often difficult. They challenge your intellect, and if you think about it, they ought to or you shouldn't be there. Who would consider giving money to a hedge fund manager they did not believe to be superior to others?

Hedge funds require both generic and specific analysis. The former includes items like assets under management, number of professional staff, and so forth, and are key to the process, but the latter drives your decision making. How does the general partner invest? Can he give you examples from this year, last year, the year before? Is the approach consistent with the general partner as a person? Essentially, can you trust him to do his best for you at all times? *Yes*, has to be the only answer to invest, and *no* means a quick exit regardless of historical returns and public reputation. If you are hesitating, that is simply another way of saying no. If you need professional assistance (and many do), get it before deciding.

There is nothing more boring than monitoring a hedge fund when returns are good, and nothing scarier or more intensive than doing so when they are bad. In either case, monitoring involves more than getting monthly performance numbers and nodding acceptance. Performance attribution is the soul of monitoring, and you can get that only by talking to or visiting the general partner regularly. If the fund does not accommodate you, it was a mistake to invest in the first place.

Risk monitoring is very valuable, but can be difficult to achieve. The average investor will be doing well to receive performance numbers and have periodic chats. The institutional investor, particularly one in a separate account, needs more and should get it. Comparisons, including comparable universes and indices, are becoming more common and available. They are useful, at the very least, as discussion points with the general partner.

Firing a manager is a judgment call that depends as much on the voice in your stomach as on the manager's performance. Poor results do not always justify termination, and good results may not be enough of a reason for keeping a manager.

Alternative investing is a part of institutional investing, though for some larger than others. Alternative investing grows and spawns new traditional asset classes like real estate and non-U.S. equity investment in developed markets, almost like a primal incubator of the future. It is unlikely hedge funds will emerge from the nursery as a traditional asset class, but for the most part they have just entered the game, and the future remains to unfold.

High net worth investors and fund of funds operators (themselves dominated by high net worth investors) currently dominate the list of hedge fund investors. The next phase of the drama is when institutions begin to discover hedge funds, and we believe that already has begun. Surely some institutional investors, particularly certain endowments, saw the need for alternative investing long ago and have progressed to hedge funds, even to in-house management of hedge fund strategies. They are the leaders, and we admire them for that. Still, we see the real institutional process accelerating over the next decade or more. Inefficiencies having been wrung out, "these elephants" will move on to new feeding grounds. For now, the herd is eyeing the area, and because of their interest, there will be a profound and permanent change in how hedge funds do business. Will they become institutionalized as did traditional equity in the 1960s? Hard to say, but the next ten years should hardly be boring.

Description of Indices Used in This Book

EACM 100^{SM}

The EACM 100 and manager universe data are equally weighted composites of audited and unaudited performance information provided by certain investment managers chosen by Evaluation Associates Capital Markets, Inc. ("EACM") pursuant to guidelines established by it (which may be amended from time to time in EACM's sole discretion). The underlying performance data is net of managers' stated fees, and reflects the performance of investment vehicle(s) represented by the investment managers to be representative of all accounts managed pursuant to a designated investment strategy. All such performance data and representations are not independently verified or approved by EACM, and EACM makes no representation as to their accuracy or completeness. EACM does not undertake to correct or to update this information in any way. Not all managers have performance data from the beginning of the period shown. Certain tables and graphs within the text refer to sectors within the EACM 100.

Compiled in 1995 and launched on January 1, 1996, the EACM history includes backdated data to January 1990. The 100 managers that comprise the index are equally divided between "niche" strategies and more broadly diversified strategies. To be included in the index, a manager generally must have at least a one-year performance record and a minimum of $20 million in assets under management. Further, managers must be open to new investment, and provide accurate and timely performance data.

Past performance is not necessarily indicative of future results. This material is intended for informational purposes only, and does not constitute an offer, solicitation or endorsement with respect to any investment strategy or vehicle.

LEHMAN BROTHERS
AGGREGATE BOND INDEX

This is a broad index, weighted by market capitalization, that includes all issues of at least $100 million par amount outstanding contained in the Lehman Brothers Government/ Corporate Bond Index, Mortgage-Backed Securities Index, and Asset-Backed Index. The Government/Corporate Bond Index is composed of all investment-grade bonds, including all publicly held U.S. Treasury or government agency debt, with at least one year to maturity. The Mortgage-Backed Securities Index includes all fixed rate securitized issues backed by mortgage pools of the Government National Mortgage Association (GNMA), Federal National Mortgage Association (FNMA), and Federal Home Loan Mortgage Corp. (FHLMC). The Asset-Backed Index is comprised of credit card, auto, and home equity loans.

MERRILL LYNCH THREE-MONTH
TREASURY BILL (T BILLS)

This is a one-security index which, at the beginning of each month, selects for inclusion the bill maturing closest to three months from that date. Returns are calculated daily from trader pricing. Any reference to these data is reprinted by permission of Merrill Lynch, Pierce, Fenner & Smith Incorporated; copyright Merrill Lynch, Pierce, Fenner& Smith Incorporated. References used herein to "cash" refer to this index, unless otherwise stated.

MORGAN STANLEY CAPITAL INTERNATIONAL EUROPE, AUSTRALIA, AND FAR EAST INDEX (MSCI EAFE)

Also a capitalization-weighted index, EAFE is an aggregate measure of approximately 1600 stocks across 22 developed nations (except the United States), the largest of which are Japan, the United Kingdom, France, and Germany. U.S. investors consider EAFE the most prominent of non-U.S. indices.

MSCI EMERGING MARKETS FREE INDEX (MSCI EMF)

This is a capitalization-weighted index of some 1000 stocks across 26 major emerging economies in Asia, Latin America, Europe, Africa, and the Middle East, major components of which are South Africa, Brazil, and Mexico. An index of stock performance of countries in the early stages of economic development, "free" means that the stocks included in EMF are available for foreigners to purchase.

STANDARD & POOR'S (S&P) 500 INDEX

A diversified, market value- or capitalization-weighted (current share price times shares outstanding) index of 500 U.S. stocks, the S&P 500 represents about 75% of the New York Stock Exchange total market capitalization. Institutions regard this measure as the key barometer of U.S. stock market performance.

APPENDIX II

Composite Performance (%)

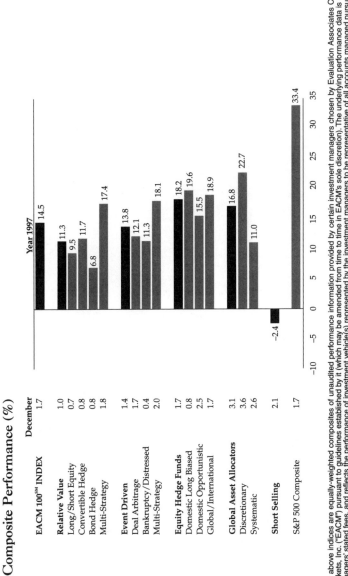

The above indices are equally-weighted composites of unaudited performance information provided by certain investment managers chosen by Evaluation Associates Capital Markets, Inc. ("EACM") pursuant to guidelines established by it (which may be amended from time to time in EACM's sole discretion). The underlying performance data is net of managers' stated fees, and reflects the performance of investment vehicle(s) represented by the investment managers to be representative of all accounts managed pursuant to a designated investment strategy. All such performance data and representations are not independently verified or approved by EACM, and EACM makes no representations as to their accuracy. EACM does not undertake to correct or to update this information in any way. Past performance is not necessarily indicative of future results. These indices are intended for informational purposes only, and do not constitute advice or an offer, solicitation or endorsement with respect to any investment strategy or vehicle.

INDEX

ABOUT THE AUTHOR

William J. Crerend is one of the pioneers in investment consulting to U.S. institutions and high net worth individuals, with a career spanning over 40 years. Crerend was a cofounder and is currently Chairman Emeritus of Evaluation Associates, one of the preeminent firms in the field. He holds a degree in economics from Niagara University and an honorary Doctor of Commercial Science from the same institution.